PRAISE FOR *SUCCES*

The vulnerability in these pages hits different than typical business books. When a CEO admits to living in a garage or a doctor shares failing tests four times, you know you're getting the unvarnished truth.
Bryan Howard | CEO of Peoplyst, Author of *The Vanguard Edge*

The stories in *Success DNA* remind us that leadership isn't about perfection— it's about growth, resilience, and lifting others.
Glenn Hopper | Author, *AI Mastery for Finance Professionals*

I'm grateful for the diverse perspectives in this anthology. No matter your industry or background, you'll find relevant insights here.
Tamara Nall | CEO & Founder, The Leading Niche

Success DNA proves that life's turbulence, bankruptcy, rejection, or career pivots, is just a layover, not a crash landing. These leaders show how to navigate setbacks with the right mindset, turning obstacles into stepping stones. It's like getting upgraded to first class after a delayed flight!
Brandon Blewett | Author, *How to Avoid Strangers on Airplanes*

This collection strikes the perfect balance between vulnerable storytelling and practical strategies. Authentic and powerful.
Shawn Johal | Business Growth Coach, Elevation Leaders, Bestselling Author of *The Happy Leader*

Success DNA is a masterclass in persistence told through lived leadership. These stories don't preach—they show how real leaders build trust, adapt through crises, and keep moving forward, even when the road disappears beneath them.
Aaron Vick | Muti-X Founder, Startup Advisor, Author of *Leaderpreneur: A Leadership Guide for Startups and Entrepreneurs & Inevitable Revolutions: Secrets and Strategies for a Successful Business*

This anthology beautifully illustrates how success isn't about avoiding challenges, but about how we respond to them.

Casel Burnett | Vice President, LODI, and International Bestselling Author of *No Regrets*

Success DNA is a timely and powerful reminder that persistence, purpose, and service are the true markers of leadership. Each story reveals the quiet grit and intentional growth that transform lives and organizations. If you're building a meaningful legacy, this book will speak directly to your journey.

Carl Grant III, Bestselling Author of *How to Live the Abundant Life* **and CEO, RainmakersGroup.io**

SUCCESS DNA

Mastering Persistence in Leadership and Life

Alinka Rutkowska • Aaron Poynton • Dr. Maria-Csilla Békés
• Dan Williams • Darius Alexander 'Dman' Ross
• Dr. Nawtej Dosanjh • Golshan Barazesh Bakhtiary
• Dr. Glen N Robison • Dr. Javier Cavada • Jochen Schwenk
• Maik Wiedenbach • Manuel R. Aragon • Paul Hepworth
• Dr. Prasad S. Kodukula, PMP, BCES • Dr. Rahul R. Prasad
• Rick Yvanovich FCMA CGMA PCC • Sharmyn Powell
• Tyrone R. Taylor • Vasanthan Ramakrishnan

Leaders
Press

ISBN **978-1-63735-387-5** (pbk)
ISBN **978-1-63735-388-2** (hcv)
ISBN **978-1-63735-389-9** (ebook)

Library of Congress Control Number: **2025909603**

TABLE OF CONTENTS

FOREWORD

Success has never been a straight line. As I reflect on my own journey from founding the publishing house releasing this book to helping hundreds of authors share their stories with the world, one quality stands out above all others: persistence.

This anthology was born from a simple yet powerful question: What keeps extraordinary individuals moving forward when obstacles seem insurmountable? The answers, as you'll discover in these pages, are as diverse as our contributors themselves.

You'll meet leaders who transformed personal crises into catalysts for growth. You'll learn from entrepreneurs who built thriving businesses from humble beginnings. You'll gain insights from experts who've navigated corporate turbulence, health challenges, and moments of profound uncertainty—emerging stronger and wiser on the other side.

What makes these stories remarkable isn't just what these individuals achieved, but how they achieved it. The medical professional who follows intuition when conventional wisdom falls short. The financial expert who overcame a troubled youth to create opportunities for others. The fitness leader who rebuilt from rock bottom to create lasting impact.

These aren't just success stories—they're roadmaps for developing your own *Success DNA*.

Each chapter offers practical wisdom for building resilience, making decisions amid uncertainty, balancing ambition with purpose, and transforming setbacks into stepping stones. Whether you're starting a business, leading a team, or seeking personal transformation, you'll find guidance that speaks directly to your challenges.

What binds these diverse perspectives together is the understanding that persistence isn't simply about enduring hardship—it's about adapting, growing, and maintaining vision even when the path forward isn't clear.

As you turn these pages, I encourage you to read not just with your mind but with your heart. Look beyond the achievements to the moments of doubt, the pivotal decisions, and the core values that guided these leaders through their darkest hours.

Then, take action. Apply these lessons to your own journey. Start small if necessary, but start today. Your own Success DNA is waiting to be activated.

Alinka Rutkowska

PART I

Defining Success

Riding Through Storms

Alinka Rutkowska

Alinka Rutkowska is a USA Today and Wall Street Journal bestselling author and the co-founder of Leaders Brands, helping entrepreneurs turn their ideas into bestsellers. She has sold hundreds of thousands of her own books and helped 220+ authors achieve major bestseller rankings, such as USA Today and the Wall Street Journal. Featured in Entrepreneur, Forbes, ABC, NBC, and Writer's Digest, she is on a mission to help 1,000 entrepreneurs publish their books by 2030.

To learn more about Alinka, Leaders Brands, and how this anthology and many of the solo books of the entrepreneurs featured within were created, visit https://www.leadersbrands.ae/.

Redefining Success in the Now

It's funny how your perception of success can shift over time. In the past, success used to be all about accomplishment: getting the best test score, landing the best-paid internship, or securing a job promotion. It was always something distant and just over the horizon, meaning that I never truly felt successful in the now; it was always about what was next. As soon as I reached one goal, it became the new normal, and I had to chase the next.

But over time, my definition of success has evolved. Today, I define success as a deep sense of fulfillment and accomplishment that comes from overcoming challenges, making a meaningful impact, and leaving a legacy that inspires others. It's not just about reaching the goal—it's about the journey. It's about going through the process, learning from the setbacks, and growing along the way.

Now, success feels much more grounded in the present. For example, when I lead a call with a potential client, it's not just about whether they sign on. True success is whether that conversation sparked a transformation in their vision. Did I help them? Did I show them what's possible? That, to me, is real impact.

Before I go to sleep, when everything quiets down, I ask myself: "What do I want?" And the answer is never far from where I already am. It's continuing

3

the life I love: leading a meaningful business, helping clients, growing my team, and, yes, riding horses (my new passion that I discovered only four years ago). That's my definition of success now—being fully present in the journey while quietly building a legacy I can be proud of.

Leadership in the Season You're In

I probably did leadership backward compared to most people. I came into a leadership role thinking there was always somebody smarter than me, so I really relied on outside expertise. Which is something you can do—and should do at certain points—but in my case, it didn't really go too well.

I took advice from people in a completely different season of life, like someone close to retirement telling me to hire for everything so I could relax and enjoy life. But when you're just getting started, that can really sink the business. So, I shifted. I went from a more laissez-faire approach to leading from the front and being deeply involved.

And then I realized something. I'm not building a business to sell, like all those "mentors" assumed. I actually want to be in it. And by being involved, I can drastically reduce costs and increase transformation for clients.

This completely changed my understanding of leadership. It became less about stepping back and more about being in the experience because, to me, success is enjoying almost every part of my day. So the key lesson? Be really careful who you take advice from—and make sure their advice fits your season, not theirs.

Persistence Starts at the Typewriter

The most significant influence on my approach to both leadership and persistence was definitely my dad. At one point in our lives, we were living in post-communist Poland—it was the late 80s—and he was applying to be a guest professor at universities in the U.S. He sent out 100 application letters. On a typewriter. Not copy-paste. One hundred letters, typed one by one.

That, to me, defined persistence. When he told me that story, I thought, "What's persistence, if not that?" So when I was applying for internships after university, that number—100—was in my mind. I don't know if I actually reached it, but I was definitely on my way.

Eventually, I got the best internship I could have imagined. It paid a full salary, which was unheard of, because people were taking internships for zero or next to nothing. I would've taken it for the experience alone, but I got both the opportunity and the pay.

So that kind of persistence has been with me from childhood. It's shaped everything. And today, I'm really careful about who I surround myself with. I join masterminds, trainings, and groups where people are aiming higher. Because you really are the average of the five people you spend the most time with.

Through the Storm to Calmer Waters

The most significant challenge was probably about two years ago. We were in this growth mindset—like we need to grow, we *have* to grow. So we invested heavily: in team members, consultants, outside training—whatever it took. The costs were very, very high. But the revenue? It just wasn't there, even though our advisors recommended we continue this way.

We kept looking ahead, thinking: it's going to have to work out. It has to. Unfortunately, it didn't. That was a big slap in the face. It really shook us.

And when money is involved, and the people you care about are involved, it's a hard hit. We didn't know what would happen. But I leaned on my closest connections—my brother and one incredible team member. There was no pity party. Just: what changes do we need to make?

We had to let people go, and these are people I couldn't imagine the company running without. But it turns out that not only did the company function, it did better. We let go of consultants and high salaries and restructured the admin. It was painful but necessary. It's what eventually turned the business around.

And yes, I had a thought: should I just walk away? Do something totally different? But I didn't. And I'm glad. Because this is what I want to do, even if I had pivoted, I probably would've come back.

Now we are sailing smoothly. We were close to drowning. But we made it. And I'm really glad we did. Persistence paid off again.

Routine as Resilience

I'm very habitual, actually. I really like having a routine. I like having structure, and I think this sort of mental discipline really allows me to deal with stuff. One of the first things I do in the morning is a five-minute guided breathing meditation. And I can *definitely* tell the difference when I do it versus when I don't.

My mornings start with getting the kids ready for school, and as any parent knows, that can be filled with all sorts of drama. If I *don't* do the meditation, my reactions are not great. I'm much more irritable. But if I *do* it, I'm much more immune to the chaos.

The other major thing for me is movement. I get much exercise. I found my passion in horses, and riding has become part of my daily rhythm. If I can get those two things done—meditation and riding—I can be hammered with calls, issues, anything, and stay calm and clear.

Even during challenging times, we operate with rhythm. We have daily and weekly team meetings, so there's structure. And that structure gives us a sense of safety. So yeah, that's what helps me stay grounded and persistent— structure, movement, and starting my day intentionally.

Leading with Structure and Support

I'm not sure if there's a perfect balance, but the structure I've built and the support I have make it possible for me to be fully present both as a leader and a mom. The other day, my nine-year-old son said, "I'm really happy your office is at home." I asked why, and he said, "Because you're here."

Even if I'm in meetings from 4:00 to 7:00 p.m. when the kids are back from school, my door is usually open. Unless it's a podcast or something where I can't be interrupted, they can walk in. Sometimes they write notes like "Can I go to the store?" or "I need money," and I'll just point to my wallet. I'm not physically with them the entire time, but I'm present.

What also helps is support. I have someone who comes in, cooks lunch and dinner, and someone who helps with cleaning. That makes a huge difference. Especially for solopreneurs, sometimes the best help you can get isn't in your business—it's having someone take care of your meals and your space so you can show up fully in both roles. That's how I make it work.

Persistence in Every Arena

I think persistence has played a key role in every area of my life. For example, I always knew I wanted kids, and I was very clear I wanted my first before turning 30. So, I started asking myself in every relationship, "Is this father material or someone who just wants to be a forever teenager?" I didn't settle. I persisted until I found the right person. That worked out.

Same thing with learning new skills like sales training. It's uncomfortable because when you're truly learning, you're outside of your comfort zone.

Same with horseback riding. Your heels need to be down, and that's not natural. Your body has to adapt. You need patience, persistence, and a willingness to grow.

The same is true in business; we had to figure out what wasn't working, cut it out, and double down on what was. There's that quote: "Remember the girl who gave up on horseback riding?" No. Nobody does. Exactly.

Anchors Through the Unknown

For me, handling uncertainty and ambiguity really comes down to the anchors I've built—those structures I can rely on. When everything around you is uncertain, you need something solid to hold on to. That could be a routine, like my five-minute morning meditation. No matter what's happening, I know I'll sit down and do it. That certainty helps me face whatever chaos the day might bring.

I also believe it's important to be your own rock. People often say, "My partner is my rock," but I don't think we should abdicate our own power like that. Still, having someone constant—whether it's a spouse, a friend, or a sibling—definitely helps. Those people who show up for you, they matter.

I've developed a mindset where I just know things will always work out. And when I look back, they always have—even if, at the time, it felt like everything was falling apart. One of our first authors once said, "Out of our darkest moments came our greatest service." That's stuck with me. Sometimes you just need to zoom out, take a broader view, and realize that what feels like the worst thing now might be exactly what leads to something great.

Keep Showing Up

To achieve success, you have to master persistence. It's not really possible without it. Nobody gets to where they want to be because they tried once. You talk to great athletes—they didn't go to the gym once and call it a day. I like to practice persistence through horseback riding. Even if the previous day wasn't great or I fell off, I went back the next day. That's how you grow—by doing it again, even when it's uncomfortable.

And it's funny, if you look at your wealth or your business progress today compared to 24 hours ago, probably nothing has changed. But if you zoom out 10 years, you'll see a massive difference. Same with your appearance— you look the same as yesterday, but not the same as a decade ago. Persistence works the same way. You keep showing up every day. And that's what gets you where you want to go.

Fail Fast, Learn Faster

One of the most valuable lessons I'd share with future leaders is this: try as many things as you can, as quickly as you can. Especially if you're not sure what you want to do, just go and experience everything. Like kids trying different sports, you don't know what sticks until you give it a real go.

I've heard of people who spent eight years studying medicine only to realize they never cared about it. They became chefs instead. So what if we speed that up? What if you figure out early on what lights you up and go all in?

You'll fail, of course, but that's part of it. Failing isn't really a failure if you learn something new. And nothing teaches better than experience. I let my kids figure things out—sometimes by touching the hot pot, but not dangerously! That's how life works. You learn, adjust, and keep going. That's success.

Choose Your Mentors Wisely

I think mentorship is important and crucial. But only if it's the right mentor. A few years ago, I remember wishing I had a parent who was also a business leader. My parents were in academia, so while my dad absolutely taught me persistence, like sending out 100 typed letters by hand to land a guest professor role, he didn't have the business experience I could ask about.

So I sought mentors. Throughout my career, there were different people I learned from. But I've realized that sometimes having the wrong mentor is worse than having no mentor at all. I joined a group for business owners making seven figures. It was something I aspired to do, and once I got there, I was thrilled to join. But most of the people were much older, in a completely different season of life. Their advice? Remove yourself from the business and set it up to sell. That didn't apply to me. I followed it, and it almost sank the ship.

It's like horseback riding. If your trainer teaches you the wrong thing, you'd be better off figuring it out yourself by feel. So I've learned to be very critical about who I take advice from. One man's meat really can be another man's poison.

Motivation Comes from Passion

I don't really need to keep myself motivated; I believe it's just there. It's passion. There was a time in my life when I didn't know what I wanted to do, and that's when it was hard. But once you figure that part out, staying motivated doesn't take effort anymore. I don't wake up in the morning, dragging myself out of bed thinking, "Why does work start so early?" or "Do I really have to do this today?" I actually enjoy it. It's something I look forward to.

That's why I'm also very intentional about surrounding myself with a self-driven team. Managing people who constantly need external motivation is draining, and it just adds unnecessary complexity, especially when you're already dealing with uncertainty and ambiguity in business. So, what is my way of staying motivated and persistent? Choose a field where you don't have to force it, where it feels natural. Then it doesn't feel like work at all.

Growth in the Saddle

I think the place I've grown the most personally, outside of business, is through horseback riding. I only started four years ago, which is kind of pretty late. Now, I own two horses and take part in show jumping competitions. One of my horses is very young, and typically, you wouldn't ride such a young horse unless you've been riding for years. But I go every day. That's persistence. It's not a once-a-week thing for me, and I'm very serious about it.

Horseback riding is fascinating because you're dealing with an animal that feels everything you feel. If you're scared, the horse becomes scared too. It's a prey animal, and its defense mechanism is to run. So you really have to regulate your emotions. You can't fake confidence. If you're nervous, the horse senses it immediately.

There are so many leadership metaphors there. If you're not the leader, the horse takes over. Same in business—if you're not leading, someone else is, and they may take things in a completely different direction.

Having this passion outside of work keeps me grounded. It builds emotional strength and keeps me balanced. If you're only doing one thing, you become vulnerable. Everyone needs something meaningful outside of work that builds you, and for me, that's horses.

Full Circle

Looking back, I realize success was never a destination—it was the act of continuing…of showing up. I want to grow into a person who can lead, persist, and stay present even through storms.

That girl chasing gold stars and job titles? She's still here, but she's quieter now—wiser. She's traded finish lines for footprints, understanding that true success lives not just in achievement but in alignment. It's riding the horse even after falling. It's leading the business not to sell, but to serve. It's asking, "What do I want?" and realizing the answer is already all around me.

Success, I've learned, isn't out there. It's now. It's here. It's built one intentional day at a time—and above all, it belongs to those who persist.

The Ripple Effect: Leadership Through Elevation

Sharmyn Powell

Sharmyn Powell's central banking career spans over 25 years at the Eastern Caribbean Central Bank (ECCB). During her tenure, she has performed in multiple supervisory and management roles. In 2016, the ECCB appointed her as their first Chief Risk Officer, responsible for the development and implementation of the Enterprise Risk Management function. She also led the ECCB's Central Bank Digital Currency (CBDC) pilot project, DCash.

Insights Magazine recently recognized Sharmyn as one of the 10 Most Inspiring Leaders in Risk Management. CIO Today recognized her as one of the top 5 Leaders in Fintech driving impact in 2025. Earlier this year, she was awarded by CToday as a global luminary who will make 2025 exceptional as a fintech leader. Sharmyn has participated in various global panels focused on risk management and central bank digital currencies. She also initiated a discussion series on LinkedIn focused on risk management in the public sector. She continues to be a key contributor in her leadership role at the ECCB.

An accountant by profession, Sharmyn is a Fellow of the Association of Chartered Certified Accountants (FCCA) and also holds the designations of Chartered Director and Audit Committee Certified, among other certifications.

S uccess is about establishing and attaining both personal goals and career targets. On a personal level, I measure success by my ability to achieve my goals in relation to professional development, financial security, spirituality, or contributing to the success of others. Each time I accomplish one of these goals, it's another step up the ladder of success.

As a leader, I continually challenge myself to be better. One yardstick I use to measure success is whether I have inspired at least 80% of the people I've led, or even those I haven't directly supervised, to pursue excellence.

Beyond my abilities, the greatest measure of my success in leadership is attaining professional maturity and becoming comfortable with the leadership of those I once led. It's recognizing that leadership is also about learning and understanding that team members can teach valuable lessons.

How My Understanding of Leadership Evolved

Early in my career, I associated leadership with job titles and seniority. Very seldom did I assert myself, thinking leadership belonged only to those in authority.

Through my involvement in extra-curricular activities and workplace committees, that perspective changed over time. In the workplace, I observed that leaders weren't always the most senior people in the room. Further, some persons who didn't emerge as leaders in the office environment stood out in other settings—on the field of play or in social settings. I recognized that leadership was often shaped by the environment and individual strengths.

Leadership requires attributes such as effective communication, emotional intelligence, consistency, and vision combined with technical skills, experience, and competence. People often say leaders are born, but good leadership comes from experience and the application of lessons learned.

Now, I have adopted the philosophy that leadership is not about being in charge, but rather about how you support the team. The true test of leadership is how others see you.

The Biggest Influences on My Leadership and Persistence

My approach to leadership has been driven by my innate desire for continuous learning and helping people to get better at what they do. I embrace opportunities to share my knowledge and experience while learning from the experiences of others.

Although I didn't always consider myself a leader, my approach and interactions often resulted in me being elevated to leadership positions, both professionally and socially; specific to my career at the Eastern Caribbean Central Bank (ECCB), I have been significantly influenced by my peers and supervisors, particularly the executive management, and the opportunities that propelled my leadership journey.

As I became more rooted in leadership, I continually received feedback from those I supervised, interacted with, and even those indirectly impacted by my leadership. That feedback has fueled my desire to continually improve as a leader. My drive comes from a passion to grow and the strong support system I have had.

Strategies for Maintaining Persistence in Adversity

Adversity can be viewed as a setback or an opportunity to course-correct. Over time, I've recognized that to overcome adversity, you first have to believe in what you have to offer. Beyond that, any contribution made should be well-founded and effectively communicated. I do my best to anchor my input in extensive research relevant to the subject area, not emotions, which can break down the leadership structure.

My main strategy is to present recommendations as points for consideration rather than imposing my ideas on others. I also try to ensure my contributions are contextual by drawing on comparable experiences.

Another source of adversity is dealing with difficult people. Experience has shown that many defiant behaviors stem from a lack of awareness or a need to be heard, and encouraging inclusion and creating a safe space to offer constructive feedback can help. However, there are instances where a definitive ruling is necessary. The key is finding that delicate balance and knowing when to be inclusive and when to take a firmer approach.

Finding Balance Between Leadership and Personal Life

For a long time, I struggled with work-life balance. My passion for excellence and maintaining high standards often meant sacrificing personal time to complete tasks, usually working late into the night without hesitation.

In large part, parenthood changed that perspective. I shifted my mindset, recognizing that I wasn't just responsible for my work anymore; I had a son whose life would be shaped by my actions, my presence, and, more importantly, my absence. One moment that stood out was when he brought to my attention that, despite my efforts, my priorities were still skewed to my 'day job.' I thought I was handling things well, but he showed me there was more I needed to do and why. That was a pivotal moment.

Beyond my responsibilities as a parent, I recognized that work-life balance wasn't just a buzz phrase—it was a necessity. Success at the expense of mental, emotional, and physical wellness is counterproductive. The lingering regrets of missing time with loved ones or important milestones forced me to re-evaluate my priorities. Now, I have made a conscious decision to take at least two weeks off twice per year, unplugging from work and leadership roles—limited phone calls, computers, emails—anything 'work related.' I also make time to engage in activities that fulfill my spiritual, social, emotional, and psychological needs, allowing me to rejuvenate, reflect, and realign my future goals.

Additionally, I have embraced the need for self-prioritization. For years, my focus was on my son's well-being and success, deferring personal aspirations to ensure he had what was needed. Now that he has transitioned to adulthood and is pursuing his own path, I can pivot to prioritizing my interests and focus more on myself.

Turning Failure Into a Lesson for Growth

While pursuing my professional accounting certification, I failed one particular exam miserably, and this caused me tremendous mental stress. It was the first time I had ever experienced such academic failure.

I was forced to face what I knew to be the source of my failure: it was not the difficulty of the exam—I simply had not prepared adequately. I had to accept responsibility for my shortcomings. But instead of letting failure define me, I used it as motivation. I retook the exam and aced it!

This is an experience that has stayed with me, serving as a reminder that failure is not the end—it's a push to do better. I often share this lesson with those I lead, including my son, reinforcing the importance of adequate preparation, commitment, and perseverance. Acknowledging failure, learning from it, and pushing forward can ultimately lead to success.

The Power of Persistence in My Career and Personal Life

In my work environment, persistence has been key in influencing policy and procedural changes. Understandably, there have been instances where I faced resistance stemming from differences in perspectives. However, my persistence, approach, and ability to present convincing arguments have enabled me to successfully influence change in various areas.

Beyond my organization, persistence has helped me expand my network and has given me increased exposure. The recent global recognition for my work in risk management and fintech was a direct result of my persistence and commitment to excellence.

Additionally, I continually receive feedback from people who have been inspired by my journey and my interactions with them; this inspires me to persevere, even in difficult moments. The realization that my example motivates others to achieve their goals gives me the push to keep going.

Persistence has helped me to help others, and it has given me the drive to reach the next level.

Mastering Persistence and Achieving Success

As an aspiring leader, one foundational thought is that failure, while difficult, is an opportunity for self-assessment and should be seen as a stepping stone to future success. There are always multiple ways to tackle a problem, so I urge people not to dwell on problems, no matter how daunting they may be. Stay focused on the ultimate goal, regroup, and persevere. Every setback presents an opportunity for a greater comeback—this has been my experience.

Success is a never-ending journey, not a destination that ends when you arrive; continuous work is necessary. Equally important, small victories along the way should not be trivialized. The focus tends to be on the significant achievements, but small victories are stepping stones that can be launching pads to push forward.

Another key point is that, although success is personal, it cannot be achieved alone. In keeping with the adage "It takes a village to raise a child," success requires encouragement, knowledge exchange, feedback, and support. It is therefore always important to show gratitude to all who contributed to the success.

True success is less about reaching the top and more about bringing others along. Success is even more meaningful when you help others succeed.

A Valuable Lesson for Future Leaders

The road to success will always come with distractions and detractors. Failure is inevitable along the way, but it should never define an individual.

Success requires deliberate effort, commitment, and a genuine desire to succeed.

Most importantly, it's never too late to start your success journey. Some people think, "I'm too old" or "Too much time has passed," but countless examples have shown that once you put your mind to it and truly commit to the work, success is possible.

The Impact of Mentorship and Support on My Success

Mentorship and support systems have been critical elements in my success journey. They have provided encouragement, guidance, access to information, and engagements I wouldn't have otherwise been exposed to.

I benefited from colleagues, family members, and a circle of friends who have provided encouragement throughout my journey. They have truly inspired me and stood by me along the way.

From a mentorship perspective, one of the most crucial influences on my success has been the executive management of the ECCB. Building on the foundation established in the earlier years, my career at the bank advanced significantly in the last 10 years, starting with my appointment as Chief Risk Officer and later as the leader of the Central Bank Digital Currency Pilot Project. These opportunities catapulted my career in ways I had not previously contemplated.

The support I received from the Executive Committee not only opened doors for knowledge expansion but also created extensive networking opportunities and outreach initiatives that contributed significantly to my success.

These opportunities created visibility and positioned me to expand my reach even further, including my contribution to this anthology.

Staying Motivated and Maintaining Persistence

Staying motivated is not always easy because of the many detractors and those instances when things don't go as planned. Those times when I've been challenged, my commitment to excellence and my passion for what I do have kept me going.

A big part of my motivation comes from recognition for my efforts and, more importantly, feedback from people inspired by my journey. Knowing that others pay attention and have been positively impacted by what I do drives my determination to continue.

I believe that motivating others through your own story to begin their journey to success creates a moral obligation to keep going. There will always be challenges and pitfalls, but the key is not succumbing to the negativity and moving forward in the best way possible.

The Vision That Keeps Me Driven

My desire to make an impact that causes others to aspire to leadership is a source of inspiration.

Coming from a small island in a relatively unknown part of the world, the notion that through my work, I can give visibility and open opportunities for others motivates me. That prospect keeps me pushing through challenges and setbacks.

Being regarded as someone who can pave the way for others is also a source of motivation. My ultimate vision is to leave a legacy that others can learn from and be inspired to achieve their own success.

Growth Through Persistence

Through persistence, my approach to personal challenges and difficult situations has evolved. In the past, I sometimes shied away from such situations, feeling inadequate. Now, I feel more equipped to navigate challenges directly and effectively.

Additionally, being more open and sharing my journey has been a personal breakthrough. This has not only shaped my career but has also helped my personal growth.

Finally, persistence has also pushed me outside of my comfort zone. A prime example is my current assignment at the BIS Innovation Hub in Switzerland. Coming from the Caribbean, moving thousands of miles away to an unfamiliar environment with no family or support system was a huge adjustment. However, drawing on my exposure and varied experiences, I concluded: "I can do this." I continue to write my story as my leadership journey continues.

Brick by Brick: Building True Success

Rick Yvanovich
FCMA CGMA FCPA MSc CCMP CCMC CBC MCH PCC

Rick is an exceptional business coach with a remarkable track record of guiding companies and individuals to unparalleled success. With his extensive experience in business and coaching, and a multimillion-dollar company serving clients in 80 countries, including top hotel chains and Fortune 500 companies, Rick empowers his clients to turn their visions into actionable strategies. This global reach extends to Vietnam, where Rick has established a formidable presence through his involvement in numerous organizations and his status as one of the longest-serving expats in the country. With over 40 years of experience across diverse industries—accounting, IT, talent, and oil & gas, Rick is a seasoned veteran in the business world. A sought-after speaker and a thought leader, Rick combines business acumen with his impressive coaching expertise to help others achieve extraordinary success.

Social Media
https://www.linkedin.com/in/rickyvanovich/
https://www.youtube.com/c/RickYvanovich
https://x.com/RickYvanovich
https://www.facebook.com/yvanovich
https://www.instagram.com/RICKYVANOVICH2/

Websites
https://www.rickyvanovich.com/
https://www.trginternational.com/
https://greatpeopleinside.com/

> *"I've learned that people will forget what you said, people will forget what you did, but people will never forget how you made them feel."*
> —Maya Angelou

For years, I believed success was about hitting milestones—until I found myself achieving goals yet feeling unfulfilled. Have you ever hit a major goal only to ask, "What now?" That's when I redefined success, not as a finish line, but as a journey of balanced fulfillment. Today, success means aligning every aspect of my life with my purpose and values. My purpose is clear: to inspire and empower humans for balanced fulfillment. This guiding principle shapes every decision I make, every action I take, and every person I seek to uplift.

Fortifying Your Castle: Balancing Your Way Toward True Success

> "The key to success is balance. Without it, even the most successful structure will collapse."
> —Rick Yvanovich

Success is about *balanced fulfillment*, not just achieving goals. It's a lifelong process of *intentionally* building, refining, and maintaining harmony across all aspects of life. It's not a binary choice between personal and professional, work and life—such separations are artificial.

In my book, *Business as UnUsual* (BAUU), I use building a Castle as a metaphor for success—one that is strong, resilient, and continuously evolving. And balance comes from ensuring that all elements of our Castle are developed and aligned. At the heart of the Castle is the **Inner Keep**, made up of four **Towers—Purpose, Life Force, Mind,** and **Self**—which form the foundation of who we are. Below the Inner Keep lies the **Dungeon**, symbolizing the deep work of **self-reflection** and **coaching**.

Beyond the Inner Keep, the **Great Hall** represents **community, culture,** and **leadership**, shaping how we connect and influence others. The **Stables** and **Treasury** reflect **transformation, satisfaction,** and **financial well-being**, ensuring long-term sustainability.

My vision is to build a life of balance and meaning, where every element of the Castle—**purpose, life force, mind, self, leadership, community, finances,** and **transformation**—is aligned. I've expressed this vision through goals like writing BAUU, mentoring future leaders, and inspiring people to align their lives. Beyond achieving milestones, my true motivation lies in contributing, growing, and making a lasting impact. I keep moving forward because I know that every action I take today lays another brick toward building a stronger, more balanced Castle.

Success Is Like Building a Castle—It's Built for the Long Run

"Success isn't a trophy you win; it's the Castle you build—brick by brick, with balance, purpose, and intention."
—Rick Yvanovich

Building a Castle takes time—it's not something that happens overnight. Each stone is placed with intention, and each building is reinforced through experience. Just as a Castle isn't constructed in a day, neither is a life of success and fulfillment. It requires ongoing effort, care, and alignment to ensure that every part stands strong and serves its purpose.

Life Force plays a critical role in keeping you going. Like a battery, it fuels your ability to act. That's why I apply **HERBS** (Health, Energy, Rest, Balance, Stress) to maintain physical and mental well-being and ensure I have the energy and resilience to keep showing up day after day. Just as a Castle requires ongoing maintenance, so does our Life Force. Regular attention and recharging are needed to remain strong.

"Take care of your body. It's the only place you have to live."
—Jim Rohn

I embrace every small victory, continue growing, and always create with intention. Structured reflection helps me regularly review each part of my Castle, ensuring that I stay aligned with my purpose and values. Balance does not mean you prioritize one thing over the other; it's about giving thoughtful attention to all areas of life.

In leadership, success isn't just about results—it's about *empowering others* to grow, make better decisions, and create sustainable success on their own terms. It's about ensuring that the people I lead and mentor achieve balance, not just higher achievement. True success in life, like building a Castle, means continuously growing while maintaining harmony in every part of your foundation.

A Pivotal Moment That Shaped My Leadership Philosophy

"People don't care how much you know until they know how much you care."
—Theodore Roosevelt

In my journey as a business owner, this transformative moment came when I shifted from being a numbers-driven accountant to embracing a people-first business philosophy. I realized that the key to leadership lies in understanding and uplifting people, emphasizing values such as adaptability, empathy, and collaboration.

The longevity of an organization is influenced by its people, as exemplified in the Japanese concept of *shinise*, which refers to long-standing businesses in Japan that have successfully adapted to modern times while preserving their core values. Japanese corporate culture values longevity and sustainability, reflected in practices such as *kaizen* or continuous improvement, *ikigai* or reason for being or what makes one's life truly worthwhile, and *wabi-sabi* or the appreciation of imperfection. Many Japanese family businesses emphasize long-term sustainability through thoughtful succession planning, ensuring each generation builds upon the last.

Shinise represents a company that lasts for generations, sustained by successive generations of people ensuring its continued success. I apply this concept to my organization by motivating individuals to keep the company thriving for years and decades to come. My leadership focus is not only on progress and growth but also on sustainability—keeping people motivated and ensuring the company remains a place where employees enjoy working. The most important aspect revolves around people, as their actions, work ethic, and operations are directly reflected in the company's performance. Make sure the right people are in the right roles.

The Influences Behind My Leadership and Persistence

My mentors influenced my approach to leadership and persistence. One of them is Marshall Goldsmith, author of *The Earned Life* and a pioneering leadership coach. I feel privileged to have been coached by him, having attended many of his workshops and events, and read many of his books. I try to emulate him, which is why I have published BAUU, offering much knowledge to people.

Another mentor of mine is Simon Sinek, a motivational speaker, acclaimed author, and organizational consultant. He has made significant contributions to leadership, inspiring people to uncover their purpose and profoundly shaping their thinking. Another person who has greatly influenced me is Dr. Peter Chee, a highly respected executive coach, author, and the President and CEO of ITD World, a multinational corporation dedicated to transforming leaders and organizations. With over 33 years of experience in coaching and developing leaders from more than 80 countries, he has played a pivotal role in guiding me toward coaching and personal growth. He has helped me deepen and accelerate my belief in the importance of developing people.

Mentorship has always been invaluable to me. A turning point was working with Dr. Peter Chee during a Certified Coaching and Mentoring Professional (CCMP) course, helping me clarify my life purpose. This newfound clarity permeated every facet of my leadership, highlighting the effectiveness of guidance and support systems.

How to Stay Persistent When Facing Adversity

Persistence thrives on clarity, structure, and accountability. One important strategy is using daily active goals (DAGs) and scoring. I track my goals daily, scoring myself either at the end of the day or the following morning. This practice ensures accountability and supports *kaizen* (continuous improvement).

Other key strategies include accountability and coaching, *kaizen*, mindfulness and reflection, and clarity and alignment. I engage multiple coaches as needed for specific challenges. *Kaizen* is my second core value, and I apply it every day, focusing on small, consistent progress. I use mindfulness to stay present and recalibrate, even amidst chaos, as it helps me manage stress and make better decisions under pressure. Lastly, I practice clarity in my life purpose and ensure alignment with it. These strategies create a system where persistence isn't just reliant on willpower. Instead, it becomes a structured, measurable, and sustainable practice.

An accountant by profession, I tend to be cautious and risk-averse, which is why I am more reactive rather than proactive. However, over time, I have realized that being proactive is better for mitigating risks. Thinking ahead, considering all possible scenarios, and having backup plans are essential for effectively managing challenges.

Remaining curious and proactively seeking where changes are likely to occur is another important strategy. Understanding these changes and their potential impacts allows me to evaluate options and choose the best course of action.

Taking action, even imperfect action, creates momentum. Inaction, on the other hand, guarantees stagnation. Change and adversity require making choices and moving forward. Inaction is often the worst decision. By taking steps, I can evaluate if the situation is improving. If I've made a mistake, I can always adjust or make a different decision.

Failure Is Not a Reflection of One's Worth

"I have not failed. I've just found 10,000 ways that won't work."
—Thomas Edison

A recent and deeply personal failure I experienced was not passing the International Coaching Federation's Professional Certified Coach (PCC) exam on my first attempt. I had scheduled the exam right after Christmas, leaving myself no time to review or prepare. Failing the exam dealt a serious blow to my ego, as I had prided myself on my credentials. I seriously considered giving up, with my self-worth as a coach diminished, despite rationally knowing that it was "just another coaching certification."

My coach and mentors helped put this experience into proper perspective, reminding me that failure wasn't the end of my journey but rather an opportunity to learn and improve. I decided to retake the exam, this time, setting aside a long weekend for studying, and gave it my all. When I passed, it proved that preparation and persistence truly pay off. And that failure doesn't define one's worth; rather, it serves as a stepping stone to growth. Even seasoned leaders can benefit from this crucial lesson.

How Persistence Shaped My Career and Personal Life

Passing the ICF's PCC exam clearly demonstrated that perseverance is the cornerstone of my journey. Expanding TRG International across several countries also required perseverance and relentless effort, particularly during economic downturns and unforeseen obstacles. Although setbacks sometimes felt overwhelming, staying persistent and true to my purpose and values allowed me to adapt, evolve, and continue growing.

This persistence has profoundly shaped who I am, not just as a leader but also as a person. It has, for instance, taught me the importance of humility and resilience. It helped me reframe my failure to pass the ICF's PCC exam on my first attempt as an opportunity. This experience reinforced the growth that comes from embracing discomfort and learning through setbacks. It has also made me a more grounded, self-aware, and empathetic individual—qualities that influence every aspect of my life, including health, relationships, and personal fulfillment.

Handling Uncertainty and Ambiguity

I have learned to approach uncertainty with curiosity, persistence, and optimism. I explore, search for solutions, and refuse to give up until the obstacle is overcome—this reflects my commitment to finding a way forward, whatever the circumstances. For instance, the COVID-19 pandemic truly tested my persistence. Our business had to pivot quickly, and instead of getting stuck in uncertainty, I focused on what we could control. Rather than dwelling on the chaos, we embraced adaptability, leveraged technology, and prioritized the well-being of our team. I remained consistently optimistic, always seeking positives and opportunities amidst the disruption.

Writing the book, *Business as UnUsual*, was one such opportunity. People kept saying, "When we get back to business as usual," but I knew there was no going back—only moving forward. That motivated me to write BAUU, challenging outdated thinking and empowering people to thrive even in uncertainty. Staying solution-focused, embracing change, and maintaining an optimistic outlook have been key to navigating uncertainty, not just in business but also in life.

My Advice to Future Leaders on Persistence and Success

Success isn't just about achieving one's goals—it's about building something meaningful and long-lasting. As I've shared, I see my journey as building my Castle. The Inner Keep of this Castle is supported by the Towers of Purpose, Life Force, Mind, and Self, each providing strength and direction. If one of these is neglected, the Castle becomes unbalanced, making it harder to grow and thrive. Achieving balance across all areas ensures resilience and long-term fulfillment.

Remember, balance is key while being persistent. Success isn't about building endlessly but about building wisely and intentionally, ensuring every part of your Castle remains strong and harmonious. Most importantly, as the architect of your Castle, shape your future with purpose, resilience, and balance.

Final Thoughts

Persistence is more than just a characteristic—it's a lifestyle. It reflects a commitment to continue moving forward, even in the face of uncertainty. It means staying curious, optimistic, and purpose-driven while maintaining balance in every aspect of life. Success isn't about reaching a final destination or achieving perfection—it's about intentionally building a life of meaning and fulfillment. Like a Castle, success is constructed brick by brick, with each decision reinforcing your purpose, resilience, and balance. Every day presents a chance to lay another brick with intention, strengthening the foundation for a lasting legacy.

> *"Do what you can, with what you have, where you are."*
> —Theodore Roosevelt

Where will you lay your next brick today?

Redefine Success to Unlock Your True Potential

Tyrone R. Taylor

Tyrone Taylor is a seasoned entrepreneur, real estate investor and legacy builder dedicated to growing impactful businesses and helping others reach financial independence through strategic real estate investing. With a background in IT, finance, and operations, Tyrone co-founded Epcot Crenshaw in 2008, which develops clean infrastructure solutions for the food, energy, and water industries. In 2015, another calling emerged when he launched into real estate investing, determined to build a legacy of generational wealth and freedom for his family.

Through relentless persistence and strategic action, he developed his real estate business from the ground up, through hardships, to build a multi-million-dollar real estate enterprise. In 2024, Tyrone founded The Property Wealth League, a community where he mentors investors, equipping them with the tools and support necessary to build long-term wealth.

A devoted husband and father, Tyrone believes that success is about living life on your terms, aligned with your purpose, vision, and freedom. His mission is to empower others to take control of their destiny and build a life they don't need to retire from.

To learn more about Tyrone and explore opportunities for collaboration, visit www.thisistyronetaylor.com.

Redefining Success

Society teaches us that having a large bank balance, holding a prestigious job title, or living in luxury defines success. This flawed logic has led to countless millionaires living unfulfilled lives. A reality echoed in the findings of the Harvard Study of Adult Development, which found that wealth and status do not strongly correlate with long-term happiness.

When we decide that we are willing to challenge conventional wisdom and create our own version of success, an awakening happens. We realize that success doesn't follow one universal definition. It's deeply personal. The legendary poet and author Maya Angelou once said, *"Success is liking yourself, liking what you do, and liking how you do it,"* highlighting that internal

26

alignment matters more than accolades. Similarly, visionary entrepreneur and billionaire Richard Branson once defined success as *"happiness"* and emphasized that if you're having fun and enjoying what you do, you're already successful.

With this understanding, we are empowered because we then know that everything we need to become successful is woven deep within us. Throughout my life, from childhood to becoming the man I am today, my definition of success slowly revealed itself to me. I will empower you with concepts and tools to achieve this for yourself in much less time.

The Early Years: Seeds of Strength

I grew up in Philadelphia, raised by parents who embodied what it means to work hard. Despite their unrelenting work ethic, money was tight, and they were constantly forced to make tough decisions to try to stretch each dollar. However, financial struggles never defined them. My father labored long hours at blue-collar jobs, which included the graveyard shift at a manufacturing plant. No matter how exhausted he was, often left with no time to do much besides sleep before his next shift, he never complained. His example taught me that even during the toughest times, you must lead with consistency and integrity.

My mother raised me into an entrepreneur. My most vivid memories of Mom working involve her business pursuits. These included a health supplement marketing business and a food truck business that she ran for several years. Her entrepreneurial spirit was instilled in all five of her children. Growing up, she constantly stressed the importance of ownership and encouraged us to build businesses.

Real Success, Revealed

Though my parents didn't have financial wealth, they were rich in faith, service, and generosity. They selflessly gave to others, donated to the church and other charitable causes, and to this day continue to live by values that are not defined by money but by their impact. They are two of the most successful people I have ever known.

Their example taught me that real success is about legacy and alignment with one's true purpose. I grew up knowing that leaders serve and empower others to grow. Through their influence, I eventually defined my version of success, which is: living in alignment with my purpose, and having the ability to spend most of my time engaged in work and activities that fulfill and inspire me.

The Formative Years: Gaining Experience and Perspective

As a young man, I worked various jobs to support myself through college, from working security at bars to being a retirement investment advisor, and eventually becoming an engineer in the IT field. This period of my life reinforced the importance of adaptability and learning from every experience.

Working in IT, I learned that programming computers all day would not fulfill my life. My quest for fulfillment led to co-founding Epcot Crenshaw with two visionary scientists. Within the first five years, our company pioneered and patented new technologies for the beneficial reuse of biomass waste. Developments that led to major breakthroughs in agricultural and food waste management garnered global attention.

Years later, my wife and I were creating a vision for the life we wanted to build for our future family. I was forced to confront a hard truth: while I remained deeply passionate about my work, the Epcot business alone did not guarantee the future we envisioned. At the time, our success heavily depended on market and regulatory factors far beyond our control.

I realized I needed more leverage. I needed to own assets. I needed a vehicle that could support our dreams and provide generational stability. And that vehicle, for me, was real estate. The shift that would happen next was not an easy one.

Throughout life, you will be faced with pivotal moments. Ones that will eventually define you. At these times, we must choose to be the leaders of our own lives and not conform to what others might prefer. I chose to be true to myself and decided my vision was worth the risk. A decision I would make time and time again.

When Persistence Is the Only Option

Tyrone Taylor, the real estate investor, was born. However, those early days of the business were dark. We took big risks investing in expensive training programs, attended paid seminars, devoured books, frequented networking events, and consumed training videos and tapes nonstop. We couldn't risk being swayed by doubt or criticism, so we didn't share many details about the risks we were taking with friends and family. We chose to move in silence and protect our goals for the new business. Sometimes, especially when you're just getting started, you need to build momentum in silence.

Struggling to make ends meet, I worked tirelessly to find our first deal. We spent months cold-calling, mailing, and negotiating with countless property owners, only to be met with slammed doors, insults, and even threats. Meanwhile, I maintained my position as COO at Epcot. I had no choice but to embrace two full-time obligations.

To stay consistent, I strategically split each day into two workdays: corporate from morning to early evening, then real estate until 11 p.m., and many times later at night. Weekends weren't for time off; they were for ensuring I didn't fall behind. There was no work-life balance, just a working life.

There were times it felt like nothing would break through. But I stayed grounded in my purpose and the example my parents gave me: face adversity with faith and persistence.

When Persistence Pays, Double Down

After several grueling months, we closed our first deal to make a $36,000 profit. With proof of concept, we knew that we could scale the business into something special. During times of triumph, it is imperative to stay focused on your long-term vision, so you don't ease off the gas and lose momentum. We pressed on to build the business through wholesaling, flipping properties, and property management.

Remember Why You Started

As the real estate business grew, we achieved what looked like success, but it wasn't right. The property management business had enslaved us, and we were not getting closer to financial freedom. We had created a demanding job that masqueraded as a business. We decided to recommit to the vision and reinvent ourselves by pivoting from the management business to refocus entirely on building our investment portfolio. This decision would define the future of our real estate business.

From Grind to Growth: Success Principles

When I stepped fully into alignment, I was able to simplify the principles that fueled my success. These are principles I live by, and ones that have helped me unlock my potential to create a life I love.

Vision Casting: Envision the Life You Want

Success begins with vision, so you have to get clear. When I exited the property management business, I did this exact exercise. I envisioned a life of time and financial freedom with the flexibility to travel with my family throughout the year, be present in my children's everyday lives, and build a lasting legacy of profitable assets that could sustain long into the future. That vision clarified a key realization: I had to stop trading time for money. To reach financial freedom, I needed leverage that can only be created by assets that continue to earn as you sleep. That clarity reaffirmed my goal to build long-term wealth through real estate investing.

Reverse Engineer Your Path

Once your vision is clear, ask: Who must I become to live that life? You have to identify the actions, habits, and milestones that will bridge the gap. Mentorship is a critical piece of this process. Learning from those who have achieved what you desire will expedite your progress. As an entrepreneur and investor, wisdom from mentors has been invaluable for helping me avoid setbacks and losses.

Commit to Habits That Match Your Future Self

Regardless of how grand your vision is, if your daily disciplines do not align with the person you aspire to become, you will never get there. We must commit to doing whatever is necessary to advance. My mantra for this is: For Myself, For My Family, For My Legacy. Reciting it every morning helps me ground myself for the day ahead.

My morning routine is my foundation, which starts with waking up at 5:00 a.m. I hydrate, meditate to clear my mind, pray, express gratitude and read ten pages of a personal development book. Working out to maintain good health, and stimulate my energy and creativity is the last critical component. I then set 3–5 main objectives for the day and begin work, usually by 8:00 a.m. By then, I've already won the day spiritually, mentally, and physically.

Welcome Failure as Feedback

Most people seek to avoid failure, but it is essential for success. It is your job to study your failures and benefit from the lessons. Just as a baby learns balance by attempting to walk and falling repeatedly, success is built upon the wisdom gained from setbacks. Those who achieve success without encountering failure often lack the resilience and knowledge to sustain it, so I believe each failure increases our future chances of success.

Embrace the Power of Service

At some point, your mission has to grow beyond your personal goals. Humans innately find purpose and fulfillment when our contributions help others, so working to serve others will drive you to keep showing up, even when your motivation wears thin. By focusing on building for my family, my community, and others in need, I am never short of reasons to keep going when the journey gets tough.

Keep Building, and Never Settle

Today, I am fortunate to enjoy a life that I don't want to retire from. It's not perfect, but the principles shared ensure that the great days far outnumber the bad. I have the freedom to build, create, serve, and be present with the people I love. This life brings me boundless joy and experiences with my beautiful wife and our two amazing boys. This, to me, is success.

My hope is that you define success for yourself, not based on what society tells you, but on what truly fulfills you. So, keep building, keep growing, and never settle for anything less than the life you were born to lead.

The Many Facets of Success

Dr. Rahul R. Prasad

Trained as an applied physicist, Dr. Rahul Prasad is an avid photographer, explorer, traveler, and adventurer. He also utilizes his technical expertise to advise venture capital firms.

Dr. Prasad received his PhD in Applied Physics from Yale University in 1987 and has worked at Yale University, Physics International Co., Science Research Laboratory, and Alameda Applied Sciences (a company he co-founded in 1994). Most recently, he was Senior Physicist and Manager at the Lawrence Livermore National Laboratory, working on various aspects of the National Ignition Facility.

He has been an active volunteer for his alma mater, Yale University, for almost three decades, serving as the Chair of the Graduate School Alumni Association (2010–2012) and the Chair of the Yale Alumni Association Board of Governors (2016–2018).

Based in the San Francisco Bay Area, Dr. Prasad is currently President of Butterflies USA (a nonprofit raising money for marginalized children in New Delhi, India), Chairperson of the Board of Amandla Development (a nonprofit raising money for at-risk youth in Cape Town, South Africa), and investor and advisor at MVP Ventures.

Defining Success in Leadership and Life

Success is an interesting term, and it means different things in different contexts.

In life, I live by something Maya Angelou once said: "I've learned that people will forget what you said, people will forget what you did, but people will never forget how you made them feel." That, to me, is the essence of success. If I can leave people happier than they were before they met me, if I can make their lives better—whether it's my family, friends, colleagues, or the people who report to me—then I consider myself successful. It's not about wealth or status; it's about impact. If I am remembered as someone who helped people grow and who made a difference, then I've succeeded.

Leadership, though, is different. It depends on where or who you are leading. If you're leading a team or an organization, success isn't about

32

you but about them. Did they fulfill their goals? Did they grow beyond expectations? A leader's role is to push people past their perceived limits, to help them see potential they didn't realize they had.

This became clear when I led volunteer groups. Unlike paid jobs, volunteers don't show up for a paycheck—they show up because they believe in the mission. That's when I learned that real leadership isn't about authority; it's about inspiration. When people are inspired, they willingly give more, not because they have to but because they want to. That same mindset shaped my professional leadership. Inspire people, and they'll go beyond expectations—not for you, but for something bigger than themselves.

How My Leadership Philosophy Evolved

My leadership style has changed over time, shaped by two pivotal moments—one in my professional career and one in my volunteer work.

When I first stepped into leadership, I believed a leader was simply the boss. The boss sets the priorities, defines what needs to be done, allocates resources, holds meetings, and ensures the team follows through. I thought I was doing a great job managing a research project in a laboratory. Every day, I checked in, talked to the team, and occasionally, when I saw something being done differently than I would have done it, I stepped in and said, "No, let me show you how." My managers told me my team was performing well, so I assumed I was leading effectively.

Then one day, a team member pulled me aside and said, "Rahul, I've been agonizing over this for days, and I just need to say it. When you come in and not only tell us what to do but also how to do it, you make us feel like we don't know what we're doing. You're not giving us ownership." My first reaction was defensive. But as he gave me examples, I realized he was right.

It reminded me of a past job where my boss constantly rewrote my reports. Over time, I stopped putting in effort, thinking, "Why bother? He's going to rewrite it anyway." That moment hit me hard. I was doing the same thing to my team.

So I changed my approach. Instead of micromanaging, I focused on creating ownership. giving my team a stake in their work.

The second pivotal moment came when I led a volunteer group. Unlike the workplace, I had no authority and no paycheck to motivate people. The only way to lead was through inspiration. I had to make sure people were passionate about the mission.

That's when I realized that leadership isn't about forcing people into roles but matching people to what they do best. If someone disliked fundraising but loved writing, I had them write grant proposals instead. Everyone played to their strengths, and that made the organization stronger.

This philosophy carried back into my professional life. I did have the authority of a paycheck, but I found I didn't need to use it. Instead, by listening, valuing input, and empowering people, I created a culture where people wanted to work with me. Internal employees from other teams actively sought to join my group, saying, "We've heard how you lead. You listen, and you take action on what your people say."

That's real leadership. It's not about top-down control. It's about creating a culture of ownership, passion, and innovation.

The People Who Shaped My Leadership and Persistence

Persistence comes from watching those who have achieved greatness, not just in their success, but in their commitment to keep going. Maya Angelou has been a huge inspiration for me. She was a prolific writer, and despite her success, she never stopped. She could have said, "I've made it. I don't need to do more." But she kept writing—not for fame or money, but to inspire thought, change, and growth in others. That is true persistence.

Steve Jobs is another figure who influenced me, especially his desire to leave the world better than he found it. As a scientist, I like the intersection of technology and art. Science teaches me precision, but my passion for photography lets me see and create beauty in the world. My background in optics allows me to capture images differently, merging physics with artistic vision, just as Jobs merged technology with creativity.

People look up to leaders, often more than they should, but that's the reality. What we say and do matters. As leaders, we must be mindful of our influence because, whether we intend it or not, our words and actions shape those around us.

Facing Challenges and Learning Through Persistence

Like everyone, I've faced my share of challenges, particularly in my field as a scientist and researcher. Many times, I've worked on projects where we felt the answer was just within reach—that breakthrough was imminent. But the more we learned, the harder the problem became. It's because you don't know what you don't know.

In science, you form logical steps: if A happens, then B happens, then C happens, so the result must be D. But sometimes, instead of D, you get E, and that forces you to question everything. Where did we go wrong? What assumptions did we make? It's frustrating to step back instead of moving forward, but persistence is the key. If you give up, you'll never reach the discovery that's waiting on the other side.

True success comes from staying the course. If every challenge makes you quit, you'll never truly accomplish anything. Every endeavor—no matter the field—will present obstacles. Persistence means embracing the learning that comes with each challenge. That's what leads to real breakthroughs.

Strategies for Maintaining Persistence in Adversity

When I face adversity, I try to take a step back and look at the bigger picture. How does this challenge fit into my entire life? Every time I ask that, the answer becomes clear: the successes, joys, and good moments far outweigh any hardship. That perspective reminds me: this is not the end of the world. It's just another hurdle.

This mindset gives me the strength to persist. Instead of seeing adversity as a crisis, I see it as a learning opportunity. Every event, success or failure, teaches us something. The key is to understand why the challenge happened and how to move forward.

I also remind myself of a famous moment from Apollo 13. The astronauts were stranded in space, and while people at mission control listed all that was going wrong, the mission controller said, "Failure is not an option." That's exactly how I approach adversity: you don't quit, you find a way forward.

Balancing Leadership and Personal Life

My wife and I raised two kids while managing our careers, and from the beginning, we made a conscious decision that we would not be absentee parents. We committed to having dinner together, spending time as a family, and being present. The key to balance is setting priorities.

Just as leadership requires prioritization, so does personal life. If I committed to attending my child's recital, I made sure to reschedule meetings. I treated family commitments with the same importance as work deadlines. Because of that, now that my kids are grown, they appreciate the time we spent together. They knew that when they needed me, I was there.

Many people struggle with balance because they don't look at the big picture. They don't prioritize effectively. I learned early on that success does not only come from what you do but also from what you choose not to do. Sometimes we fill our schedules with easy tasks, taking time away from what truly matters.

A colleague once told me, "Work smarter, not harder. Work smarter, not longer." That means breaking tasks into smaller, manageable steps and staying focused. True balance comes from deciding what matters most—and refusing to compromise on it.

The Power of Persistence in Career and Life

Whenever I take on a leadership role, I set clear goals for success. One example that stands out is my time as Chair of the Yale Alumni Association, leading over 175,000 alumni worldwide. I wanted to create something that would engage alumni with current students—a program that would continue long after my tenure ended. I launched an initiative bringing alumni from various professions back to Yale to share career insights with students.

Ten years later, that program is still running. Seeing its growth has been a defining success, not because I ran it but because it persisted beyond me. That experience reinforced my belief that real impact comes from persistence, long-term vision, and thinking beyond yourself.

Embracing Uncertainty as a Path to Growth

When facing uncertainty, I take comfort in something an old friend once said: "This too shall pass." It's a simple phrase, but it carries great wisdom. Uncertainty is temporary. Given time, clarity will emerge.

One of the biggest periods of uncertainty in my life came when I left a small business I had co-founded. I no longer saw eye to eye with my partners, but I had no plan for what came next. It was unsettling, but I knew I had to make a change. Instead of fearing uncertainty, I embraced it. Shortly after, I was offered an opportunity at Lawrence Livermore National Laboratory, where I worked for nearly 20 years. That opportunity only came because I was willing to take the leap.

The same applies to my personal life, like when my kids were applying to college. We waited with bated breath and wondered what was going to happen. But then, I reminded myself to put in the effort and trust the process, and things will work out. Uncertainty isn't a dead end but a sign that change is coming. And change should never be feared.

The Key to Persistence and Success

Patience is key. Think about how we learn to walk. You take a step, you fall. You get up, take another step, and fall again. But you keep going. Eventually, you walk more than you fall, and soon, you're running. That same persistence applies to everything in life.

Whether it's learning a skill, growing in your career, or building strong relationships, success requires effort. Just like problems at work don't solve themselves, relationships don't thrive on their own. You have to put in the work. The key is simple: if you don't succeed at first, try again. And keep trying, because persistence is what turns failures into victories.

Staying Motivated and Maintaining Persistence

The way I stay motivated is very interesting. I like to take walks in nature. I go out with my dogs, whether it's in a park, by the sea, or by the bay— wherever I am. I take in the expanse of nature and its beauty, and it reminds me that our lives are just a tiny part of the universe. The universe has persisted for billions of years, and it didn't happen by giving up.

I also find motivation in human achievement. When I walk through a city, I look at century-old bridges and buildings built without the technology we have today, yet still standing strong. I think of the astronauts landing on the moon and how their calculations were done by hand. Neil Armstrong once said he wouldn't board the spacecraft unless the numbers were hand-checked by people he trusted.

If they could persist, why can't I? I hold onto the belief that I must leave the world better than I found it. That is why I keep going. Until I can do nothing at all, I will always strive to do more.

Closing Thoughts

On February 19, 2025, my wife and I celebrated our 40th wedding anniversary. It's a personal milestone, and it happened because of hard work, persistence, and never letting challenges derail our journey.

That's something people should remember: success doesn't happen overnight. It comes from years of dedication, overcoming struggles, and pushing forward even when things get difficult. Whether in relationships, careers, or personal growth, the key is to stay committed, work through challenges, and never lose sight of what truly matters. That's the real foundation of success.

The Learning Leader

Paul Hepworth

Paul Hepworth is a seasoned technical and organizational leader with over two decades of experience scaling high-growth startups. From founding engineer to executive, he has built and led cross-functional teams in engineering, product, and design across more than ten companies—helping them navigate the messy middle between early traction and sustainable scale.

Known for combining sharp technical insight with people-first leadership, Paul excels at diagnosing root issues—whether structural, cultural, or code-related—and turning friction into momentum. He partners closely with founders and transitional-stage leaders to evolve their organizations, build strong systems, and develop resilient, high-performing teams.

Paul's approach is grounded in curiosity, observation, and a relentless drive to figure things out—a mindset shaped early on as a teenage habit of bringing home broken things, making them work again, and selling them for a profit. He's since become a trusted advisor and catalyst for change, helping companies build not just software, but the capability to grow.

Based in Mountain View, Paul enjoys life with his wife, two dogs, and a garage full of tools. His three college-aged kids are never far from his thoughts or his group texts. He finds joy in bikes, hockey, community service, and tackling challenges others walk away from.

Defining Success

Success is defined by how continuously one persists and improves despite setbacks and challenges.

In mathematical terms, it matters more that your slope is positive than where your y-coordinate is at the current moment—time and efforts will ensure eventual success. Yes, we will encounter challenges and failures. But as long as we continue improving, we will be successful.

How Leadership Evolves

When I was young, I thought, like many do, that a leader is a person who gives out orders or is at the top of an organizational structure. However, as I grew up, I realized that being a leader is about how one acts and behaves regardless of one's position or authority. Anyone can be a leader by demonstrating leadership—taking initiative, understanding others, finding solutions, providing opportunities, and so much more. It's about looking at the bigger picture and taking ownership over your situation, your team's situation, your company, or your family's situation.

I can say that my view of leadership evolved, thanks to the influence of my father.

During a year-long stint in his career as a turnaround specialist, he always had the servant leadership mindset, and he saw himself as one who enabled other people's success. He'd go to struggling companies and support them in any way he could. My father is not the leader who ordered people around, but he helped people find their way.

My father talked to truck drivers, executives, the staff, crew, and service people so he could understand how things are going in their day-to-day work—everyone in the company. He was a leader who LISTENS to UNDERSTAND.

My father would make an effort to understand where they're coming from, what's working or not, what's the root problems, what could've been done, and so on. From there, he would collaboratively come up with solutions that were eagerly applied by the people he worked with.

Growing up, his servant leadership approach inspired me and made me think: this is how a leader should act towards his people. What my father did in his work taught me that I should also understand and support others when it's my time to lead.

Experiencing Significant Challenges That Helped Me Grow

In every success, we always experience challenges that make us doubt. However, challenges should never be seen in a bad light because this is where we learn and grow.

My significant challenge started very young when I, not knowing it at the time, struggled with dyslexia. I often misunderstood instructions and was unable to follow along with the lessons in the classroom.

But later on, I learned to use my dyslexia to persevere instead of giving up. I worked harder and asked more questions. I'd look at assignments from multiple angles and identify multiple possible interpretations of instructions and approaches. I began to accept that I needed to fail fast, get early feedback, and avoid making too many assumptions. By developing these habits, I created a long-term work ethic and an almost insatiable curiosity around how things really worked. This has helped me embrace root cause analysis and first principle thinking, which led me to ask more questions and surface core assumptions so that I can get a complete understanding of situations. As I grew up and matured, I put in more effort, worked harder, and ensured that I was more prepared for the things I needed to do.

Overall, I eventually got into the habit of not making assumptions based on what I see at first glance. When I became a software engineer and worked for different companies, I looked beyond what was in front of me. I realized as I began my profession that the dyslexia that had once held me back had prepared me to be an extremely effective knowledge worker who would instinctively be able to question and challenge assumptions and uncover opportunities. Who would have thought that a seeming disability could become an asset after years of struggle and practice?

Balancing Leadership Responsibilities

In both my personal and professional lives, leadership always boils down to the importance of understanding and supporting others, as well as what you want to accomplish together. This is why I always emphasize that you have to ask questions and understand where people are coming from, whether they're your colleagues or your family. By doing so, you can support and guide them while also providing feedback and clarity.

Managing Ambiguity

Most of life is ambiguous as we encounter situations whose outcome we don't know. The biggest opportunities in my career are the ones where the outcomes were not determined and the current risks and challenges were not fully understood. So, I jumped on those and tried to understand them by asking questions and figuring out what needed to be done. From there, I came up with actions to help make my team and company successful.

Many years ago, I joined a struggling company called UserTesting. I had used their product and saw its potential, but they had some significant technology hurdles that were holding them back. Competition had begun to grow, and they were stuck.

I knew I'd be able to understand what needed to be done by asking questions, and that's what I did. I talked to the people and listened to their concerns, suggestions, and ideas. Because of my persistence and continuous improvement mentality, as well as my ability to make the right decisions, I formed a solid team and built a solid technology. It took a lot of hard work, many failures and learning, but eventually, the company was very successful in everything that they did. Challenging ambiguous situations that seem far from perfect are the best opportunities for growth and development.

Staying Motivated and Maintaining Persistence

When we experience failures and challenges, it's easy to give up, lose motivation, and stop. But sometimes, we just have to step back and analyze what we are doing. Sometimes I have to step back and see what my priorities are. I think breaking down goals is one way to stay motivated and maintain persistence.

Recently, I experienced this when I went hiking with my son to the summit of Mount Whitney, the highest peak in the lower 48 states in the United States. Weeks before our hike, my son expressed interest in doing something challenging with me before he moved away for a couple of years. So instead of going head-on and being overwhelmed, I researched and read about experiences from other hikers. I saw there were so many things to do to prepare in order to make sure we were safe. It was almost overwhelming, but I realized that in order to be fully prepared, we need to break down our larger goals into smaller, manageable tasks. As we did so, I saw that everything we needed to do was achievable, and we understood the risks and realities better as we planned out the whole trip. Though still very physically and mentally challenging, we completed our goal safely.

Things are really hard at the beginning when we have larger goals. But once we break them down into smaller, manageable tasks, it becomes easier to achieve the bigger picture.

Building a "Horrible Version"

Another thing that I do regularly that helps increase motivation, persistence, and belief in my teams is to encourage my team to first build a "horrible version" of a project quickly. I have found that by doing this, we're able to avoid being overwhelmed by perfectionism. Often, even the best of us can be focused on building a great product, but at the same time, get pressured to make it perfect, which leads to being overwhelmed by everything. By fully committing to building a "horrible version," they are forced to think smaller, more simply, and are willing to move ahead quickly without overthinking or being concerned about what others might think. I try to reinforce this imperfection by praising pragmatism over perfectionism.

If we compare ourselves to perfection, we eliminate our enthusiasm and often our ability to achieve our goals. Knowing that most people will too often tolerate perfectionism slowing down their progress, I regularly remind my teams that the value of simplifying by building a "Horrible Solution" that we can improve is way better than becoming overwhelmed and not making any progress.

Overall, I'm a believer in knowing where you want to go, creating a vision for that, and insisting on it, and being okay with initial imperfection.

Contribution of Persistence to Personal Growth

I have a lot of different experiences in my professional life that have helped me maintain persistence and contributed to my personal growth. One of them is when I trained a stray dog, Cody. He was a beautiful dog that loved to chase squirrels or anything that moved. While an amazing dog, it needed some serious training. I signed up for a community dog training course at a local park. At first, I thought that I was going to those classes to get my dog trained, but what I quickly realized was that I was the one being trained. Once I was trained, I could then get my puppy to behave properly. I am certain that I learned more than Cody did.

I learned that if we're patient with ourselves and make practice a priority, we can learn to do anything. I ended up taking that concept and applied it to both my profession and my personal growth.

A key lesson I learned from that dog training course is to give both positive and negative feedback quickly—timing is everything. So, for instance, if I'm going to give them a treat for a reward, but they don't know what they did in order to get that, then they're not going to actually connect the behavior I wanted to reward to it. It could be worse, and it is entirely possible that they associate the reward with undesirable behavior, which I could, if not conscious of it, be training my dog to the exact opposite of what I wanted them to do.

The same is true with people. When somebody does well at work, instead of waiting for the end of the project to give feedback, I give it straight away. Giving feedback close to their action helps in letting them know that they're on the right track and it reinforces the right thing for them and for the organization. What a great lesson to learn from an unsuspecting place.

Advice and Lessons for Future Leaders

Being a leader is no easy feat, and it takes a lot of courage to be an effective one. Here are some simple lessons that you can follow.

First, I advise aspiring leaders to focus on the bigger themes, risks, and potential gaps in the projects or teams. To do this, it can be helpful to zoom in and out of the situation to maintain perspective while also understanding enough detail. This gained perspective is a way to break down a situation in a way that surfaces important insights to help eliminate being overwhelmed and identify what needs to be done first.

It's not in our nature to zoom in and out on a frequent basis. We end up zooming in for way too long sometimes, and end up getting stuck in details, or we zoom out too long and don't take enough action, or make costly assumptions. So, it's important to balance it out so we can still take more action in the long run. Zooming in and out in every discussion and needing to frame what needs to be discussed is critical.

Second, do not expect things to come easy and you must understand that success often takes years of hard work.

Nowadays, social media influencers and YouTubers make it look like success is very, very easy. However, what people don't see is the process that they use to achieve that success.

Thinking that things come easily just because you are a nice person or you want something is not true. It takes many years of hard work, striking out, and experiencing challenges to eventually get to a point where your skills are honed and your perspective is matured. As many have said, overnight successes only take about ten years. Those close to those people or situations understand this very well.

Third advice is to focus on the process of getting better and to be patient with themselves and with others. By being patient, you can focus on improving, learning, and growing. As they say, one can overestimate what they can do in a day, but often underestimate what can be done in a year. The compounding effect of continuous improvement is very real, but unfortunately, few really get to experience it.

Last, but definitely not least, it is important to recognize that everyone has challenges, so you have to keep working forward despite experiencing setbacks. Use these as opportunities to grow and learn, so you know what works, what different approaches to use, and what work ethics to retain. There is always something to be learned from opposition, difficulty, and failure. Always.

PART II

The Journey to Success

The Path to Success: Perspectives in Persistence and Success

Dr. Nawtej Dosanjh

Dr Nawtej Dosanjh is an executive business coach and a trusted adviser to executives and colleagues. He is also a distinguished leader in international higher education and co-founder of Vedere University, in Florida, USA, which is focused on AI and technology in the healthcare sector. With board, advisory board, and executive team positions across various educational institutions and charitable organizations, he has provided insights and strategic direction in several areas, including governance and content creation. In 2025, he published his first novel, A Climate of Chaos: This Parched Earth and will publish a management book about ambidextrous leadership (simultaneously maximizing being efficient and innovative) and AI. Visit his website www.iniciahub.com for more details.

Success is often measured by the accumulation of wealth, and there is nothing wrong with that. However, without an alignment to our underlying motivations, core values, aspirations, and interests, accumulating wealth may be difficult. Undertaking activities in which you have only a passing interest, or that you may dislike, for several hours a day, year after year, purely to accumulate wealth, is a heavy lift. On the other hand, doing things that you love, and/or for which there is a purpose, means that we may not even look upon these activities as work.

So, what do you love doing? What are your motivations? What is your purpose? How can the things that you love doing, with a little imagination, be turned into accumulating wealth? Where can you get help with this thinking? Who are your coaches and mentors? Olympic gold medalists, tennis champions, and the best footballers in the world have multiple coaches. There is no shame in getting help, and it's doubtful that we can even set the right goals without getting help.

How I Define Success

My personal definition of success has evolved over the years, and there have been several pivotal moments. One of those moments came almost three decades ago when my children were born. I became very motivated to become a provider for them. But there was something larger at play in my thinking. I wanted them to have successful lives, and I aspired to be a role model for being financially successful. Over time, I wanted to also demonstrate and model being personally fulfilled in every conceivable way. I worked hard on setting challenging long-term goals and working on the minute steps I would take. I started to surround myself with people who could be my coaches and those whom I could learn from.

Today, my personal definition of success is having the agency to, as far as reasonably possible, remain unaffected by external circumstances. It involves the eradication of all negative influences that can hinder personal growth or achievement. This includes discarding assumptions, which are often preconceived notions or beliefs not based on facts, allowing for more informed and objective decisions. It also requires eliminating bias, which is the tendency to favor certain ideas or people over others. Fairer and more balanced perspectives can be achieved without bias. All of this can be summed up as recognizing and avoiding self-limiting beliefs. Avoiding self-limiting beliefs is essential, as these can prevent people from taking control of their lives. It is crucial to maintain a broad self-perspective because people can only achieve what they believe is possible.

Those who are able to dismantle their self-imposed limitations and instead have unreasonably high expectations of themselves will start to find ways to take the first steps. Of course, there are conditions in the external world, such as our starting position, which impose some degree of difficulty. However, focusing on the external world and not the internal is self-limiting.

Throughout these almost 30 years, I have relied on people to help me and coach me, and I have done the same for others.

My personal view of success has evolved to include a great many other things, none of which would have been possible without first dismantling my preconceived assumptions. Today, central to my definition of success are the following:

1. To be in physical, emotional and mental good health.
2. To recognize and ensure that I do as little as possible that could be less than positive on the mental and emotional well-being of others.
3. To actively apologize when I get this wrong, even remotely.

4. To authentically and calmly be the advocate and champion for those who I see being less than positively affected.
5. To surround myself with people of high integrity.
6. To do interesting things with interesting people.

Key Influences on My Leadership Style and Persistence

Several people have significantly influenced my approach to leadership and persistence. Naturally, my parents, partner, and children have been my inspiration. And the strong relationships I've formed with my circle of friends have provided the push I needed at times. I've made a conscious effort to develop highly positive friends, as it was my goal to have loving and mutually supportive relationships.

Beyond the influence of the people in my life, education has also played a crucial role in breaking down my self-limiting beliefs and improving my self-perception. When I talk about education, it does not have to be formal education, but it does have to be proper learning. It has had a liberating effect, freeing me from the constraints imposed by self-doubt. By maintaining a positive self-concept and controlling my thoughts, I ensure that my actions remain positive.

On the journey towards success, there are significant challenges, especially for most of us who are not born into wealth, and it is important to recognize that. To overcome those challenges, I developed certain strategies and habits—some by accident and some by design—to nurture and maintain my persistence and drive.

Over the last decade or so, I've cultivated an attitude of feeling fortunate, born out of an authentic sense of gratitude, to work with the amazing people I have around me. I hope and believe they feel the same. This crucial mindset of gratitude enhances our interactions and collaborations. The mutual appreciation ensures that I'll never be disappointed with the outcome of our work. All of this stems from having good self-esteem, which makes me feel lucky to engage with others because of the positive energy they bring. This results in all of us fostering an enjoyable and productive work atmosphere.

The development of my mindset has led to my being able to address my self-concept, which has helped me regulate my thoughts. I allow myself to be human, but for the most part, I do limit negative thoughts from taking root in my mind. A positive belief system leads to positive activities that ultimately help achieve my goals.

Overcoming Failure and Key Challenges

One significant challenge I had to overcome, which is common for those pursuing their goals, is achieving the proper balance between professional and personal life. Twelve years ago, my balance was very poor, but I finally achieved it with the help of two overarching values: joy and my love for doing interesting things with interesting people. Joy is very important to me, which is why I always ensure it is present in both my personal and professional life. The second value is doing things I love with people I enjoy being around. I established a rule that if I'm not experiencing joy or doing interesting things with interesting people, I'm not going to engage.

Failure is an inevitable part of life, especially when you are serious about achieving your goals. For me, it's all about attitude. Despite the many failures I experience, I use them to propel my future. I have many regrets about a lot of things in the past, even when I've been successful. However, I don't see it as negative; instead, I use it to motivate myself to improve in areas I regret. Similarly, I use failure as motivation to keep going until I achieve what I set out to do. Persistence is essential.

Thanks to being persistent, I have experienced many positive outcomes. I've co-founded a university, assisted advisory boards and executive teams in providing strategic direction, and had the opportunity to coach and mentor truly great people. Additionally, I've created a lot of content for master's degrees and other forums. Recently, I completed writing a novel and expect to publish this as well as a management book on *ambidextrous leadership* (which is about the ability to simultaneously maximize being efficient and being innovative) next year. Overall, my career has been fantastic, having learned from my past failures, and I continue to be persistent.

Navigating Through Times of Uncertainty and Ambiguity

I experience periods of uncertainty and ambiguity, and many have asked how I handle such situations in both my personal and professional life. My answer is that part of me loves uncertainty and ambiguity because they challenge and arouse my curiosity. An unclear environment excites me because it offers an opportunity to excel, to change and to grow. Naturally, another part of me makes me feel anxious. However, I don't allow the anxiety to overwhelm me. To reduce the anxiety and ambiguity, I ask questions and find more information to enable me to move forward. A great friend, coach, colleague, and co-creator of content has been a crucial collaborator for me. And he has been so generous in acknowledging (in his writing) my part in his growth.

For instance, when I co-founded a university, it was a period of uncertainty for me. However, I viewed it as an opportunity to learn new things and to excel. I put together the right people, and we successfully navigated the process.

For aspiring leaders, mastering persistence and achieving success involves expanding their belief systems. Instead of imposing a limit on what they believe is possible, they should set unreasonably high expectations for themselves and then commit to and love the journey. Such a positive attitude can significantly impact their personal growth, relationships, and financial situation. It is based on self-image, and they should never allow the outside world to dictate their beliefs and reality.

Having mentors and support systems was vital in my success journey. I have experienced the benefits of a support system and have also provided support to others. I've served as a coach for others, helping others to improve. I was also coached by a great professor when I became an academic, who taught me how to excel at teaching master's students, who do and should demand nothing but the best. I depended on his mentorship and support, and I strongly believe that without his coaching, I would not have been as successful as a professor, which would have limited the other futures which I was able to follow.

Motivation plays a vital role in achieving success, as it helps maintain persistence. However, we all know it is a constant struggle to stay motivated. To keep myself motivated, I make it a point to work with interesting people who align with my values.

As I previously mentioned, joy is a key value for me. Engaging in activities I love, such as great conversations, fun events with friends, reading a great article or a great book, fills me with immense joy. Working on new endeavors allows me to engage in interesting thought processes with others. This is what keeps me motivated despite any challenges and setbacks I may face. I don't really see setbacks and challenges as negative any more, but rather as opportunities for doing something interesting.

An important observation I want to emphasize is that big impacts don't necessarily require large inputs. Very small changes, even a 1% improvement in a certain activity, can lead to exponential improvements or significant impacts. Slightly tweaking an activity can lead to massive success. My evolving perspective has led me to realize the importance of aligning my actions, methods, motivations, and core values.

Ambidextrous Leadership and Lessons to Share

Finally, I want to emphasize that one of the most helpful things I learned around 20 years ago was ambidextrous leadership, even though I didn't know yet what it was called at that time. I began focusing on being efficient in my work while also seeking to be creative in what I did. I then tried to optimize both simultaneously. This approach was one of the most significant factors that contributed to my career. Most of us focus on becoming very efficient or on constantly exploring new things. A few people learn how to do both simultaneously. Because of all of the things I have shared in this chapter, I was fortunate enough to do something a little bit innovative. This concept of being *ambidextrous* ultimately became my PhD.

Success comprises a number of elements, some of which I are as follows:

- Have a plan: What are the things that you love doing? How can one of these be aligned with what you do for several hours a day? How can this become an income?
- Goals: Set some goals and work out the small steps to achieve them. But more importantly, allow your goals to evolve and even change completely.
- Persistence: Commit to and love the journey and journeys; never mind the setbacks.
- Self-improvement: Constantly seek to improve oneself, learn from failures, and grow from experiences.
- Balance: Maintain a healthy balance between different aspects of life, such as work, personal relationships, and self-care.
- Positive mindset: Cultivate a positive attitude and belief system that supports one's ambitions and actions.
- Alignment with values: Ensure that actions and goals are in harmony with one's core values and principles.

- Support systems: Have mentors, friends, coaches and family who provide guidance, encouragement, and support.
- Joy and fulfillment: Find joy in the journey and derive satisfaction from both the process and the outcomes.

In conclusion, success is a personal journey, and its definition can evolve over time as one's priorities and circumstances change. I encourage everyone to define their own success and persist in achieving their self-defined goals. And ambidextrous leadership, a concept close to my heart, is an approach I want to share with those who aspire to achieve success in leadership and their careers, just as I have.

The Power of Perseverance
Golshan Barazesh Bakhtiary

Golshan Bakhtiary was born on June 17, 1990, in Masjed Soleyman, a year after the Iran-Iraq War. Her journey to success began in 2016 when a chance encounter in a Fendi store led to her participation in a regional competition to select Miss Italia 2016. This paved the way for the establishment of the Miss Persia project, which now serves as a platform for women's empowerment on a global scale.

It was a challenging journey that required considerable effort and perseverance. This included collecting five thousand personal signatures, participating in marches, and walking twenty-one kilometers barefoot. She had to overcome numerous obstacles, including cultural barriers imposed by Iran through the Ministry of Culture and circumventing sanctions imposed by the United States on Iran.

Golshan is an international beauty expert, social activist, and entrepreneur known for her commitment to promoting social change and supporting women, especially through her efforts to create the Miss Persia crown in the Miss Universe beauty pageant. Her movement led the Miss Universe organization to pay more attention to the participation of women from all countries, regardless of restrictions. She proposed the idea of Saudi women participating in Miss Universe with the help of her business partner, Mr. Zak Hawa, resulting in Saudi women entering the competition for the first time. Since then, Miss Universe has allowed women from previously restricted countries like Cuba to participate in this prestigious global competition. Though often working behind the scenes, Golshan's movement has achieved significant global impact.

Her resilience kept her going despite early setbacks. Her tenacious spirit eventually caught the attention of the Miss Universe Organization, which asked her to travel for extended consultations.

Golshan will receive the Women's Global Leadership Award at the Universal Women's Leadership Forum in September 2025.

https://www.instagram.com/golshanbakhtiaryofficial

https://www.linkedin.com/in/golshan-bakhtiary-814b3b153/

Living with Resilience and Insight

I have always believed that I was born to be a leader. I have always sought challenges that were difficult, demanding, and creative—what better way than to fight for my country, Iran, and all countries suffering from restrictions and discrimination? It took us seven years to overcome various obstacles, including my country's opposition to Iranian women competing in such events, while the United States opposed it due to UN sanctions on Iran. Most of our efforts, including the 21-kilometer barefoot walk in Italy and the collection of 5,000 signatures, were done in person rather than online, with video documentation of all signatures collected. Now, in my eighth year of efforts, I have a broader vision for my project: creating a platform where women from the Middle East can compete for top global titles and where deserving women can prepare for global leadership roles through annual events and positive work.

I am no stranger to hardship. During the COVID-19 pandemic, I lost my job and was forced to live in a two-meter motorcycle garage on the basement level. My journey began early—at three years old, I started reading and writing Persian with my mother's encouragement. By age five, I was attending professional painting classes. Throughout my education, I participated in various competitions, sometimes winning first place, sometimes second. At just thirteen, I became the youngest artistic director for Iran's most important theater and cinema festival, "Fajr."

A Journey Beyond Barriers

For me, success has always meant having clear goals and focusing my efforts on achieving them. Working hard and concentrating on my objectives gives me a sense of purpose and enthusiasm. I learned this invaluable lesson from my parents. My father worked at the National Iranian Oil Company, and from a young age, I remember the smell of paint from his artistic and carpentry projects. Every day after work, he passionately engaged in meaningful activities. At fourteen, he seized the opportunity to work in the oil company by passing the entrance exam for "Talented Iranian Boys," and through dedication, he became a leading engineer in his field. My mother, too, was always creating literary and philosophical works, recognized as a prominent professor of literature and poetry.

I believe success is an inspiring mindset that views challenges as opportunities for learning and growth. This perspective includes the courage to tackle difficult tasks, step out of one's comfort zone, and transcend perceived limitations. I apply this mindset in both leadership and personal life. Focusing on valuable efforts, such as mastering new skills or creating impactful works, is integral to this journey.

Success is about living with purpose, continual growth, and relentless effort. This path encompasses pursuing joy and fulfillment in every step toward a goal. Each step forward is a victory, motivating me to keep moving ahead.

As a leader, I never share my struggles with my family. I believe working quietly and striving independently is far more valuable. Parents naturally love their children and cannot bear to see them struggle, often either discouraging their paths or rushing to support them, which prevents them from developing a stronger character.

After completing each task, I inform my family of my accomplishment and share the challenges I overcame. This approach helps me have my family's support while fostering pride and achievement within myself.

Lessons from My Childhood

Throughout my journey, my understanding of leadership has evolved as I learned to harness my creativity and talents despite limitations. Finding solutions, even when resources weren't readily available, has always been essential for me. Growing up, I watched my father rise early, work diligently, and still find time to pursue his passions.

These moments shaped my philosophy of life and approach to leadership. A pivotal experience occurred when I was fifteen and wanted to create a new game or sport. When others told me it was too expensive, I felt underestimated simply because I was a young girl. This taught me the importance of finding solutions and remaining adaptable when pursuing goals.

I grew up just a year after the Iran-Iraq War ended, in an environment with limited health facilities, schools, and resources. Creativity and ingenuity were vital for solving the problems we faced. Witnessing my father's hard work while he still made time for his interests profoundly impacted me, encouraging me to be resilient, resourceful, and persistent in finding solutions.

Beyond my father, I drew inspiration from scientists, athletes, and other remarkable figures whose biographies I read throughout my childhood and teenage years.

My mother often recounts how, as a child, I would hide under the dining table listening to conversations, scribbling strange letters nobody could decipher. On my first day of school, I sat under the classroom table, absorbing sounds and refusing to emerge until my mother arrived. The teacher announced that any first-grader who could write their name on the blackboard would receive an excellent grade in spelling. The classroom fell silent. At that moment, I quietly rose from under the table and raised my hand, and that was the beginning of a new chapter for me!

From then on, whenever I needed to concentrate, I would hide under tables or behind cabinets to focus on reading various biographies. At fifteen, I read one of my brother's university geology textbooks three times! Despite my family's wonderful support, my environment didn't provide the same opportunities as other countries. Feeling dissatisfied with my progress, I strived to discover new pathways by delving into more books.

These experiences taught me humility, resilience, and the importance of continuous learning. They shaped me into a leader who understands that true strength lies not only in personal success but also in lifting others as we navigate our journeys together.

From Immigrant Struggles to Entrepreneurial Success

As the only daughter in my family, I had a comfortable life in my country, but from childhood, I dreamed of leaving my homeland. This dream motivated me even when my family opposed it. After years of determination, I finally convinced them to let me emigrate.

A significant challenge I faced was being homeless as an immigrant student. Without a job or steady food, I lived in a garage without internet access. I had to be resourceful, taking screenshots from books because I couldn't read them online. One of those books inspired me about personal and business growth.

I spent every penny my father sent on educational investments, beauty pageants, and networking with important people in Italy. I participated in more than twenty competitions, providing everything from gala dresses to mental coaching. When my family opposed my participation, I made a bold choice: I would no longer accept their financial support for my dreams.

Instead, I pretended their money was spent on living expenses and education while it was actually fueling my aspirations.

This decision meant working tirelessly to pay for basic needs. My father's college scholarship supported my education, but it often left little for other expenses. Every sacrifice brought me closer to my dream, teaching me resourcefulness and flexibility.

I remember one rainy night when water flooded the garage, preventing me from sleeping. It was uncomfortable, but I was accustomed to hardship. I viewed it as an opportunity to grow through resourcefulness and creativity.

During the COVID-19 lockdown, I solved my financial problems by selling dresses on Facebook and investing the proceeds in cryptocurrency. After the lockdown, I played the Hang drum on the street, earning money and gaining social media popularity. I also did self-portrait photography, sometimes using just my cell phone inside the garage. Outside, I wore beautiful dresses, despite returning to that garage later.

Turning Failures Into Opportunities

Those challenging times ended when I found restaurant work again. I saved money by eating only once daily and soon used my savings to start a business.

I never informed my family about my hardships, telling them only that I was doing well. I've practiced solving problems independently and restraining tears, which has made me smarter and more resilient. I believe positive thinking allows us to achieve anything we want. To maintain positive energy, I meditate, even for just a minute, and visualize my goals. I imagined opening a restaurant, a cocktail bar, and my brand—all of which came true after dedicated work.

I've experienced failure several times. Recently, as National Director of Miss Universe for Persia, I worked with our beauty queen for two years, hoping to achieve the Miss Universe 2024 crown. When she didn't make the top thirty, I was disappointed. After three weeks of reflection, I realized we needed a strategy change, which became the positive outcome of that failure.

Perseverance and hard work have led to my successes. When many said it was impossible for my country to compete in Miss Universe, I persisted. When the organization's owner invited me to travel from East to West with them, I agreed, visiting Thailand, Turkey, El Salvador, Mexico, and many other countries in just five months.

My advice to future leaders is to be creative and remember they're part of a team. We can't succeed alone—people must help each other and learn from one another. Always remain humble and recognize that everyone has something to teach us.

You can find mentors simply by looking around you. Hearing someone's story can be educational, regardless of who they are. A stranger discussing politics might teach you about culture; someone talking about wealth or poverty might offer valuable insights if you simply listen.

I stay motivated by remembering that nothing is impossible if you truly want it. Maintaining positivity has been my guiding philosophy. Without my positive outlook and work ethic, I wouldn't have achieved my goals.

If I had only one piece of advice, it would be to remain persistent and hardworking. Many people try something seven times and then give up, missing opportunities they could have achieved with perseverance. If I could describe myself in one word, it would be "hardworking."

Balancing Leadership with Personal Life

I've always strived for balance. My organizer contains notes about work, my business, painting, and other activities, alongside personal priorities. Each day, I address both leadership responsibilities and self-care. Writing things down helps me organize tasks while maintaining balance. My busy life allows for only a few close friends alongside many social acquaintances—exactly how I prefer it, as I wouldn't have much time for close friends if I had too many.

In a Nutshell: Persistence and Hard Work Lead to Success

After reflecting on success while writing this chapter, I feel I can achieve anything. The timeframe varies with the goal—becoming a country's president might take decades, while other objectives require less time. The key is to remain persistent in moving toward any goal, to work hard, and to stay positive despite obstacles. Persistence, hard work, and a positive mindset are essential for overcoming challenges and achieving dreams. Keep striving forward with determination and belief.

Leadership in Couple Therapy: Navigating Love, Gender, and Cultural Connections

Dr. Maria-Csilla Békés

Born in 1970, Dr. Békés grew up in Transylvania, Romania, as a Hungarian-speaking, German-born minority in a communist dictatorship. This experience continues to shape her with intergenerational identity questions. In 1990, she emigrated to Germany. Dr. Békés pursued her medical studies in Germany, England, and Hungary and completed her doctorate in Vienna.

With a passion for languages, she speaks six languages and has traveled to forty-seven countries. In addition to her love for kickboxing, which she practiced for eight years, Dr. Békés is also an accomplished writer, with her debut short film receiving six awards worldwide. Art has always been an integral part of her life.

As a specialist in psychiatry and psychotherapy, Dr. Békés focuses on couples and sex therapy. She is a recognized expert, frequently featured in the media, and is currently writing a German guide for couples and trans people. Her therapeutic approach emphasizes careful guidance, supporting individuals and couples with tact as they work towards greater satisfaction in their lives, gently but determinedly.

Dr. Békés has lived in Zurich, Switzerland, for 25 years, where she has two grown sons. Her marriage is both unique and transcultural, built on a deep connection with her very conservative yet highly progressive Moroccan husband.

paarberatung-kanton-zurich.ch

http://www.csillabekes.ch/#/

https://bekescsilla.hu

Adventure or Madness? My Start Into the Unknown

My success story started the way every good story should start, with adventure, danger, and a bit of madness. The scene was a whole continent–South America. Following long years of study and a doctorate in medicine, I started my specialist training in psychiatry at a clinic in Cologne. But after a year, I was inexorably drawn overseas. I had to leave. On January 1, 2000, I was in Buenos Aires with a suitcase full of dreams and a vague idea that Europe might not see me for a while.

In Patagonia, I met a fascinating WHO (World Health Organization) team of social workers, nurses, doctors, lawyers, and volunteers dedicated to ensuring the preservation of the medicinal culture of the Mapuche Indians, who were the main losers in the upheaval of the continent by the Conquista. Uprooted, deprived of rights and work, many families fell into a web of poverty, alcoholism, and violence.

Mate, Mistrust, and Courage: A Gringo Learns Trust

My task was to track down Mapuche families in the Patagonian forest and provide them with food, medicine, and a bit of confidence. One of my first encounters was with a family suffering from leprosy. Clearly, there were also recognizable traces of domestic violence. Of course, as a Gringo doctor, I was initially received with suspicion. There was this thing called the *matetee*: an earthenware cup full of tea leaves, water, and sugar, with a single metal tube that everyone drank from one after another. The cup was passed around in a circle as a greeting and an introduction to conversation. It was unthinkable not to drink, but a voice inside me screamed: "Leprosy! Stop!"

From Leprosy to Love: The Beginning of a Therapeutic Career

What could I do? The seconds passed like hours. I was 30 years old, single, and had no plan to start a family yet. The motto of intercultural psychiatry is to immerse oneself in a foreign culture to help. So I drank. The metal tube hung around my mouth, and the decision was made. I didn't get leprosy, but I won the trust of the family and began my career in family and couples therapy and transcultural psychiatry. It was the entry into a world that was to affect me deeply.

From Chaos to Happiness: Leadership with Heart and Insight

Today, more than two decades later, I am the proud owner of a couple and sex therapy practice in Zurich. My approach is to lead, not like a CEO or a manager, but as a professional guide accompanying people on the way to happiness. I lead people out of toxic relationships and into joyfulness. I lead people out of toxic relationships and into loving happiness. Trans people in particular were already close to my heart when terms like gender dysphoria didn't even appear in scientific marginal notes. While practicing the art of careful leadership, I learned to listen, accept worldviews, and not impose rules.

Gender, Boundaries, and Big Decisions

Early on, I had some *aha!* experiences on my way from a psychiatrist to a manager. Let me tell you about one of them: I was the accompanying psychiatrist of a trans woman, who later became known throughout Europe for her media-effective and committed work for trans people. That was 25 years ago. We are still in contact. Two or three years ago, she confessed to me that she regretted the gender-matching operations. In her own words, she said she was too young, too enthusiastic, and too impatient. Now she felt she would be happier if she had only undergone hormone therapy. I was new to this field then and tried to just work with her empathetically and accept her wishes. To be honest, an inner struggle was already raging within me: How will I forbid, allow, influence, and lead carefully? My leadership ideology was still in its infancy at that time. I have learned that especially insecure personalities seek advice and help from psychiatrists. One should not be dominant, but practice considered leadership through the chaos of problems.

Learning from the Best: A Tribute to the Queen of Couples Therapy

At this point, I would like to make a grateful and respectful tribute to a wonderful woman with a great personality: my teacher and supervisor at the Training Institute for Systemic Couple and Sex Therapy in Switzerland. She was a mature, dominant, and extremely intelligent woman with high-status allure. She was ruthless and challenging. She taught us that a weeping psychiatrist is not a good psychiatrist. Clients want compassion but not pity. Most importantly, they need professional, therapeutic guidance. She continued to pave the way for me long after the training was completed and, unfortunately, died far too young. How ironic that this highly intelligent woman had dementia.

Hungarian Serenity: Life Lessons with Humor

My Hungarian roots are faithful companions on my way as a gentle, therapeutic guide. This small, special country with its turbulent history teaches humor and serenity: "The only certainty is that nothing is certain," "Never say never," and "There are no difficulties, just adventures." These pearls of wisdom shaped me, and that's how I raised my children.

"Is This an Adventure, Mom?" A Leadership Test in a Bus Accident

My elder son and I took the bus to the mountains. He was three years old, comfortably stretched out on a seat in a deep sleep. I was half asleep, enjoying the stunning scenery. Then suddenly, everything was literally upside down, and there was wailing, screaming, and chaos. Instinctively, I pulled my son to me to protect him from the unidentified peril. The bus had skidded and rolled down the slope.

When I opened my eyes, it became clear: The message standing on the roof. There was blood, screams, and panic everywhere–it was very dramatic. My son woke up, looked around, and asked: "Mom, is this another adventure?" My answer, of course, was: "Yes, but a bit of a fail." He didn't scream, tremble, or cling to my neck. Instead, he just turned over and went back to sleep. The message was understood: "Mom, you are doing well. I feel safe." At that moment, I was proud. I'd passed the leadership test.

Success: Cards, Calls, Compliments, and a Free Life

Let's stick to successes. As a professional in the management of families and couples, when I receive Christmas cards from former clients in the jungle of their issues or if someone who was in therapy with me calls after fifteen years because they need help again—since our work together was valued at the time so much that they would not go to anyone else–I feel joy and success. Success in life is to be satisfied. This is the opinion of the majority. But please do not confuse this with happiness. Happiness is like a chance lover—you often don't notice it until it slams the door on the way out of your life.

My own private success is extraordinary and affects my way of life as a professional care leader for couples and families. On New Year's Eve years ago, I set out to lead a life in which I could determine my own sleep rhythm, not dependent on family, social obligations, or following the day-night rhythm of nature. My rhythm. At first, this sounds crazy and simplistic, but it means that I am economically independent enough to design my daily routine. This is financial success. It also means that I can sleep soundly during the day because a clear conscience and fun at work are my companions. And finally, I hear that my private environment–family, friends, neighbors– accepts and respects my rest time. This is love, respect, and generosity. A multi-faceted success.

The Cinema Trick: Shifting Perspectives for Better Problem Solving

My secret for dealing with adverse circumstances in the careful management of couples and families is the cinema trick. In the front row, dramas seem deafening, unmanageable, and overwhelming. From the back row, everything becomes quieter, clearer, and more bearable. When faced with adversity, this playful strategy helps you see things from an eagle's perspective—from above, in context, and not from a worm's perspective, where the edge of the well already represents the horizon. A balanced alternation between the worm's and the eagle's perspective from the back row in the cinema… that's problem-solving at its best. Sometimes I am direct and decisive, but careful leadership is not small talk; it is a courageous decision to achieve self-knowledge.

Life's Treasure Box: Humor and Loyalty in Everyday Life

Let's take a quick look inside Aunt Jutta's nonsense box. In my private life, I often need protection and an adventurous journey for its own sake. The most important motto for the protection of my private life is, "no professional deformation." No leadership ambitions in friendships, raising children, and partnerships. At parties and meetings with friends, I am often overwhelmed with questions about love relationships. My reply is: "Let's set up the practice alarm clock and listen to the money flowing into the cash register." A pinch of humor and loyalty to yourself–the best chill recipe for leisure.

A Date with the Dark Side: Leadership Starts with Yourself

The fact that our thoughts influence our actions and state of mind is now common knowledge, not only for managers. Nevertheless, a surprising number of successful people struggle with mental health problems. For example, Michael Jackson, the German rap kings Sido and Bushido, opera diva Maria Callas, and professional footballer Francisco Rodríguez all had to deal with depression, panic attacks, or excessive drug use. The list is endless. But why?

Many successful people come from either poor backgrounds or average, petty-bourgeois families. What unites them? A grandiose vision. But with every success, the gap between the origin-I and the goal-I grows. These inner gaps—between the person you were and the one you want to become—are dangerous. They create tension, suffering, and a kind of suction effect that pulls you down again and again, like an invisible gravity. So far, so good, but how should one react? Does success necessarily have to go hand in hand with suffering?

A tip for you: as a leader, do not neglect your dark side. Regularly allocate a few free hours to maintain the relationship with this often unnoticed part of yourself. Sounds weird? I regularly invite my shady side to dinner. Yes, really! I set the table for two, sit down, and take my time to deal with her.

Be kind to your dark side—not only as a leader but also the person behind it. After all, she ushers you to your psychological, mental, and physical well-being.

Perseverance, Please! Success Recipes from the Alchemy Kitchen

Well, as we are already dispensing wisdom, praising chill recipes, success pills, prescribing happiness syrup, and clarity tablets, let's put together a homemade recipe for successful leadership in this cave of alchemy: perseverance is necessary, but in moderation because it can be bitter. Fighting is inevitable, although it tends to upset your stomach. Perseverance is a crucial component of a solid, pleasant fragrance. Consistency is indispensable as a solvent for all the other components. That would be my recipe for your success and mine.

There is also the playful psycho variant: success comes and stays when it feels comfortable with you. If everything is a struggle, success feels bad and leaves your life. Of course, perseverance, consistency, and above all, a clear vision are essential for success. Visionaries have been either persecuted or idolized in many cultures. Half vision does not work and leads only to half success. If you have a clear vision, coupled with courage, calm, and consistency, success feels good and stays with you!

Empowerment Economics: How Lifting Others Builds Success

Vasanthan Ramakrishnan

Vasanthan Ramakrishnan is an entrepreneur, nonprofit leader, and author with a passion for empowering teams and redefining success for young entrepreneurs. As the youngest recipient of an honorary doctorate at 26, his journey spans award-winning initiatives like Feminist Pen Foundation, where he led diverse teams across seven countries, to his current role as CEO of Ascend, a thriving seven-figure business with a 50-person team serving Fortune 100 clients from all around the world. His upcoming book, "Breaking 9 to 5: Playbook for the EB-1A Einstein Visa (Free Resources Included)," offers practical insights drawn from his extensive experience in nonprofit work and corporate leadership, inspiring others to unlock their full potential.

Redefining Success and Leadership

Success is not measured by your title or your net worth but by the fulfillment found in your personal growth and the positive impact you **make** on others. In my view, success comes from a journey of self-improvement and from helping others achieve their own potential. You are probably wondering what "helping others achieve their own potential" has to do with your personal or **business** success. It seemed **counterproductive** to me at first, but I learned that you win by helping the people around you win, especially when it comes to your business. Whether it is a tech company you founded or a busy hot dog stand you own, your success really comes down to how well your employees perform. And I am not talking about vanity metrics like how many LeetCode problems your best developer can solve in a day or how fast your BI team can churn out a report. I am talking about the big picture here: taking care of your customers. I am sure you have come across the words of successful entrepreneurs like **J.W. Marriott Jr.** and Richard Branson, who say, "Take care of your employees and they will take care of your customers." That is not just a saying; it was the truth in my case. In over half a decade of entrepreneurship that **took me from a solo founder to a CEO managing multiple businesses with teams of 50**

or more people across the world, I have always found success when I put my team first.

In this chapter, I will share how my understanding of leadership evolved through personal trials and moments of deep reflection. My aim is to offer insights and practical lessons for young entrepreneurs who are setting out on their own paths. The focus is on creating a story that connects personal experiences with the broader idea of success, one that celebrates growth, humility, and the courage to redefine what it means to lead.

The Evolution of My Leadership Philosophy

In my early **twenties**, I believed that leadership meant having all the answers and directing every step with absolute certainty. This was a time when I had seen moderate success for entrepreneurs at my age. I had just **co-purchased** my first house with my mother, and I wanted to create a clothing brand that I would sell online and in-store. **E-commerce** was still new, as storefront sales in retail brought better margins than online selling because most people were not used to buying online and ended up returning products after trying them once or twice. So, I banded together a crew of my cousins and friends and launched "Handkrafted" (handcrafted with a "k"). Against a wise team member's advice to go completely online, I ended up leasing a cheap **satellite location for the brand's storefront.** But what I did not know at the time was that sales directly depended on location, foot traffic around the store, the buying power and fashion preferences of the people around the **ZIP code, cost of goods manufactured (COGM),** cost of logistics, and many other factors. We went bankrupt **within six months** of launch and had to sell our inventory at half the price to people we knew, taking a huge loss.

All that time, I used to think that a leader's role was to set the vision and expect immediate compliance from the team, no matter how impractical that vision appeared. Luckily, my team was made up of people I knew, so they did not leave me after the **"big fail."** They stayed to teach me a big lesson about effective leadership, and my perspective began to shift. I realized that effective leadership was not about controlling every detail but about empowering others to contribute their best work. I had team members who excelled at selling but struggled with design, and I had others who were excellent at forecasting and problem-solving but were not as strong in execution. I slowly started to observe and listen to the team's unique strengths and weaknesses and began to leverage their strengths instead of focusing on their weaknesses. I started to empower rather than simply order people around. I learned that leadership is about fostering an environment where everyone feels valued and has the opportunity to shine. This change in mindset led me to place greater trust in my team and focus on collaborative problem-solving.

Two years later, I launched Feminist Pen Foundation, a four-time award-winning human **rights** nonprofit organization that, at its peak, had fifty team members from eight countries and **earned** me two honorary doctorates in humanities. I even received an endorsement from a **Nobel Peace Prize laureate** who praised my unique nonprofit leadership style. Mentorship and shared learning played a crucial role in my transformation. I found guidance in conversations with experienced mentors who stressed the importance of accountability and mutual support. Working with diverse teams across different cultures taught me that listening and understanding are as important as making decisions. In my journey from a solo founder to a CEO managing a **seven-figure** business, I discovered that leadership flourishes when there is a collective commitment to success.

Persistence in the Face of Adversity: Lessons from Rejection

The journey toward building a successful business rarely follows a straight line. My early ventures taught me that setbacks are not endpoints but stepping stones toward growth. In the beginning, with Handkrafted, I learned this lesson the hard way. But rather than seeing this as a complete failure, I realized it was an opportunity to learn what I needed to improve. I had people who believed in me and were willing to take another chance on my leadership. This failure didn't mean that I was no longer a founder again. I became one, maybe not the next day, but two years later, with Feminist Pen Foundation.

These early experiences laid the foundation for the creation of Ascend HSI Advisory Partners, my current company, which launched three years after Feminist Pen Foundation. Ascend emerged from the resolve to build something robust and innovative. I applied the lessons learned from Handkrafted and Feminist Pen Foundation, focusing on building a company culture that thrives on collaboration and adaptability, one that empowers every team member to contribute their strengths. At Ascend, every rejection or unexpected challenge has become an opportunity to innovate, refine our strategies, and serve our clients better. Today, my almost fifty-person team from two countries solves, manages and serves 100+ clients from Fortune 100 companies seamlessly, not because I told them to, but because they love to do so. They take pride in serving our clients with accountability and true passion towards the work they do.

For young entrepreneurs, the message is clear: embrace failure and rejection as part of the journey. Each obstacle is an opportunity to learn and improve, but don't do that alone. The setbacks I experienced pushed me to adopt a more resilient mindset and to focus on empowering my team.

Balancing Leadership Responsibilities with Personal Life

Balancing the demands of leading a company with personal well-being is an ongoing challenge that has taught me to value intentionality in both areas. Early in my journey, the focus was solely on growing the business, often at the expense of personal time and relationships. Over time, I learned that sustainable success comes from investing in oneself and in the people around you.

When I launched Feminist Pen Foundation and later Ascend, the pace was relentless. We were moving from signing three to four five-figure contracts a month to doing that volume in a day. However, I found that effective leadership required more than just business acumen; it demanded an understanding of human needs. I began to set clear boundaries for work and personal life, creating space for family, friends, and personal growth. For instance, I scheduled daily periods for deep work and dedicated evenings to reconnecting with loved ones. One of the top game changers that helped me balance work-life effectively is my four-day work week. While I have twelve-hour work days through the week, I get an extra day to relax, recharge, and spend time with family and friends. That makes a monumental difference in my daily mood and helps me do more meaningful work with the less time I have.

I also discovered the importance of delegating tasks and trusting capable team members to handle critical responsibilities. This allowed me to step back, reflect, and focus on strategic decisions without becoming overwhelmed by the minutiae of everyday operations. Building a reliable team meant that each individual felt empowered to make decisions and contribute meaningfully to the company's goals.

For me, balance is not achieved by dividing time equally but by prioritizing what matters most in the moment. I learned to adjust my schedule based on urgent business needs while protecting personal time as a non-negotiable commitment. This flexibility has enriched my life by reducing stress and increasing overall satisfaction, both personally and professionally.

By embracing a work-life integration approach, I have been able to lead with clarity and energy. The success of Ascend and my other ventures has shown me that nurturing personal relationships and maintaining self-care are not obstacles to success; they are essential ingredients in building a resilient, innovative team and a fulfilling life.

Overcoming Uncertainty and Embracing Adaptability

Navigating uncertainty has been an inevitable part of my leadership journey. At Ascend, I encountered periods of ambiguity that forced me to rethink established strategies. There were moments when shifting market dynamics or sudden changes in regulatory requirements left us without a clear path forward. Rather than waiting for certainty, I chose to embrace the unknown. I encouraged my team to approach these challenges with a problem-solving mindset, breaking down complex issues into manageable parts and exploring multiple solutions.

In these situations, I found that staying calm and relying on my team was essential. I began to take on a data-driven approach, gathering insights from various experts and listening to team members who brought diverse perspectives. I learned to trust the process of experimentation. Not every decision yielded immediate success, but each attempt provided valuable feedback that guided our next steps.

This approach helped us develop contingency plans and flexible strategies that allowed my company to navigate through tough times. I realized that adaptability is not just about making quick decisions; it is about fostering a culture where change is seen as an opportunity to grow and improve. By building an environment that supports continuous learning and innovation, I ensured that uncertainty became a space for creativity rather than a source of fear.

For anyone facing uncertainty, the key is to remain agile and maintain focus on the long-term vision. Embrace the possibility of multiple outcomes and be prepared to pivot when necessary. Every challenge holds a lesson, and by learning from each experience, you build the resilience needed to overcome future obstacles.

Key Lessons and Words of Wisdom for Future Leaders

Leadership is a journey of continuous learning and adaptation. One valuable lesson I have learned is that persistence in the face of setbacks is not a weakness but a strength. As the saying goes, **"Success is a marathon, not a sprint."** Embrace every challenge as an opportunity to grow and refine your strategies. I encourage young entrepreneurs to focus on empowering their teams, recognizing that genuine success emerges when each member contributes fully.

Another lesson is the importance of building trust through open communication and accountability. Leaders who listen carefully and value the input of their teams create an environment where innovative ideas can flourish. Remember that every setback carries a lesson that can transform your approach to decision-making. It is essential to cultivate a culture where feedback is welcomed and learning is a shared goal.

Effective leadership is also rooted in humility. Acknowledging that no one has all the answers allows for collaboration and fosters a spirit of collective problem-solving. As you embark on your leadership journey, remain adaptable, seek guidance from mentors, and always be prepared to adjust your vision as circumstances change. Focus on long-term growth rather than short-term victories, and let every experience add to your resilience and wisdom.

Conclusion: The Ongoing Journey of Success DNA

My journey has taught me that success is not an endpoint but an evolving process that requires courage, determination, and a commitment to lifting others as you climb. By empowering those around you, you pave the way for mutual success, whether you are managing a tech startup or a small local business.

I hope the lessons shared in this chapter inspire you to view challenges as opportunities and to lead with both strength and compassion. As you navigate your own path, remember that true leadership comes from the ability to inspire, listen, and create an environment where every individual can excel. Keep building, keep learning, and never underestimate the power of a united team in achieving extraordinary success.

Forward Motion in a
Non-linear World

Dan Williams

CEO, ONELIFE Senior Living

Dan Williams is a pioneering force in senior living with over 25 years of transformative leadership experience. His portfolio encompasses the management of 100+ stabilized communities, 30+ new developments, and numerous successful turnaround projects.

His executive achievements include scaling two organizations significantly prior to starting his own company. After founding Ally Senior Living, he merged with ONELIFE Senior Living, where he now serves as CEO.

Currently holding interests in over 20 senior housing communities nationwide, Dan leverages his extensive experience as CEO, partner, principal, and COO. He frequently contributes to industry discussions through Senior Housing News, Seniors Housing Business magazine, and the National Investment Center.

As an executive board member of the American Seniors Housing Association, Dan continues driving industry innovation and standards. His expertise in scaling organizations, strategic mergers and acquisitions, and operational excellence has established him as an authoritative voice in senior living's future.

https://www.linkedin.com/in/dan-d-williams/

onelifeseniorliving.com

The Moment of Truth

It was about 3:00 p.m. when I checked into my Sacramento hotel room, 3,000 miles away from a decision that would test every strand of my leadership DNA. Hurricane Ian was barreling toward Tampa, Florida, and while all models had shown our Memory Care Community would be safe, my worst fear materialized on The Weather Channel. The hurricane had shifted, putting our memory care community, just 75 miles south of Tampa and near the coast, directly in the eye's path. Sixty seniors with Alzheimer's disease were counting on us to keep them safe, and they would soon face one of the worst storm surges on record.

The easiest path would have been to wait to see if the models would shift again. But leadership, I've learned, rarely follows the easy path. Moving elderly residents with late-stage Alzheimer's comes with significant risks, but watching those satellite images and seeing one of the most powerful hurricanes in history gathering strength, I made the call to evacuate immediately. From my hotel room across the country, I had to trust completely in our local team's ability to handle this emergency.

Within minutes, our team orchestrated what seemed impossible. They coordinated transportation, packed essential medications and equipment, and carefully loaded each resident. Our staff members left their own homes and families behind to ensure our residents reached safety in Orlando. They made it just in time—the hurricane hit with devastating force shortly after, leaving catastrophic destruction in its wake, including our community.

Evolution of My Success DNA

Looking back at that Hurricane Ian experience now, I can see how it crystallized everything I've learned about building successful organizations. Like genetic code that activates under pressure, true success emerges most powerfully during critical moments. It wasn't about policies or procedures—it was about people who understood their purpose: protecting those in their care while building something greater than themselves.

Just as DNA adapts and evolves through generations, my understanding of leadership has been shaped through experiences. While I once thought it was about control and authority, my journey from my first job as a live-in assistant manager in an independent living community helping take care of 110 seniors to an organizational leader has shown that lasting success comes from empowering others and trusting in their capabilities.

This crisis not only tested our leadership but also validated our approach to building successful communities. The trust we'd built, the systems we'd developed, and the teams we'd grown all came together. It demonstrated how solid foundations—built through years of prioritizing both resident care and team development—enable not just crisis management but sustainable success.

The DNA of Decision-Making

I can still hear the gasping sound. It was a quiet afternoon in our independent living community when chaos erupted in the dining room. One of our residents—a retired school teacher I'd talked with just that morning—was choking on a rib bone. Her face was turning blue, her eyes wide with panic, and her hands flailing.

In that moment, everything became crystal clear and terrifyingly complicated at once. I wasn't licensed to perform the Heimlich maneuver—in fact, as crazy as it sounds, regulations explicitly prohibited "assisting" residents in an independent living community by an unlicensed person. A manager was pulling at my arm, urgently reminding me about protocols and liability. But watching this woman struggling for air, seeing the terror in her eyes, regulations seemed meaningless.

"You can't do this—you're not certified!" the manager warned. But just like that moment in my Sacramento hotel room years later during Hurricane Ian, sometimes leadership means trusting your instincts when lives are at stake. I stepped forward, positioned myself behind her chair, and performed the Heimlich maneuver. The rib bone dislodged, and she drew in a desperate, beautiful breath of air.

This is where having a great mentor made all the difference. After the ambulance left and things calmed down, I called my supervisor, Russell, my hands were still shaking, and I was worried about breaking protocol. His response shaped my leadership DNA forever: "You never go wrong doing the right thing." While this wisdom wasn't original to Russell, his timing in sharing it was perfect—simple, clear, and exactly what I needed to hear. That wisdom would echo years later during Hurricane Ian when our team had to balance safety protocols with the urgent need to evacuate.

Habits and Strategies That Reinforce Success

Time has consistently reinforced what makes both leadership and success possible: daily habits that build trust and capability over time. Like a success blueprint embedded in our organizational DNA, these practices have helped transform challenging situations into growth opportunities.

Daily reflection isn't just a practice—it's a success multiplier. Whether processing a crisis decision from a Sacramento hotel room or reviewing monthly financial results, taking time to assess what's working has consistently led to better outcomes. Some days are too busy for formal reflection, but the practice always finds its way back, like a compass pointing toward growth.

The value of honest feedback is another constant in my leadership DNA. I actively seek it, not because it's a best practice, but because every experience has shown that straightforward conversations about improvement are invaluable. Those uncomfortable moments when someone points out your blind spots? They've consistently proven to be catalysts for growth. Without this kind of honest feedback, it's impossible to truly discern what's working and what isn't.

A Pattern of Persistence

Every crisis and every challenge has reinforced a fundamental truth: persistence isn't about blind determination—it's about maintaining clarity of purpose while building sustainable success. During Hurricane Ian, our team's persistence wasn't driven by sheer willpower—it was powered by years of developing systems that work, teams that care, and communities that thrive.

Early in my career, I sat down and wrote out eight specific goals— ambitious targets that made me both excited and nervous to look at. Today, I've achieved six of those eight goals, but it didn't happen through force of will alone. Each success came from maintaining a clear purpose and adjusting course when needed—rarely straight, but always forward.

This pattern emerged during my early career climb. Each rejection— "not enough experience," "too young," "overqualified"—taught me something crucial about persistence. It wasn't about proving others wrong; it was about staying true to my vision while learning from each experience.

Building and Reinforcing Trust

The Hurricane Ian evacuation powerfully reaffirmed what I've learned about success—it's built on a foundation of trust, proven in moments both big and small. When I had to trust our team from 3,000 miles away, it wasn't blind faith. It was confidence built on countless smaller moments where they'd demonstrated their capabilities, leading to consistently strong outcomes for our residents and communities.

Trust, like DNA, replicates itself throughout an organization. When leaders consistently demonstrate trustworthiness, it becomes part of the organizational genetic code. Whether it's a crisis moment like the choking incident or daily operational decisions, the principle remains the same: trust is earned through consistent action, reinforced through transparent communication, and proven in moments of challenge.

The Power of Purpose and Results

Looking at our success blueprint today, something becomes crystal clear: motivation isn't just about personal drive or achievements. It's about finding that sweet spot where organizational success aligns perfectly with serving others. When I found senior living, or maybe when it found me, this alignment clicked into place. Here was an industry where building successful communities meant making a real difference in people's lives.

Each community we've turned around, every team we've developed, and all the lives we've touched reflect this dual focus on purpose and results. It's not just about the metrics, though our growth numbers and resident satisfaction scores tell a compelling story—it's about creating environments where success multiplies, where doing well means doing good.

Vision and Long-Term Motivation

Success in leadership, like DNA, follows patterns. Throughout my career, three elements have consistently proven essential: clear goals, genuine belief in your purpose, and the persistence to see things through. During our Hurricane Ian evacuation, these elements came together perfectly—clear purpose, authentic commitment, and unwavering follow-through.

Those eight goals I set early in my career? Six were achieved, while two are still in progress. But here's what experience has repeatedly shown—it's not about checking boxes. It's about having a clear vision that guides your decisions, especially during challenging times. When you know exactly where you're headed, each setback becomes a setup for a comeback.

The most powerful confirmation of this has been seeing how authentic conviction spreads through an organization. You can't fake it—people know the real thing when they see it. When you truly believe in where you're going, that authenticity becomes contagious. It transforms individual effort into collective purpose.

Conclusion: Rarely Straight, but Always Forward

Everything I've experienced—from that first dramatic choking incident to Hurricane Ian, from early career setbacks to building thriving communities—

has reinforced this fundamental truth: success isn't about having a perfect track record. It's about maintaining forward momentum, even when the path twists and turns. Another mentor of mine, Aaron, always reminded me, "rarely straight, but always forward."

The journey from jobless, broke, and sleeping on a friend's apartment floor to leading successful organizations hasn't been linear. But each step, each decision, and each challenge overcome has added another strand to our success DNA. We've built communities where residents receive exceptional care, where team members grow professionally, and where doing the right thing drives sustainable results.

Henry Ford's wisdom that "Whether you think you can or you think you can't, you're right" has been proven true countless times. Your mindset isn't just part of the equation—it's often the decisive factor between giving up and breaking through. This mindset has helped us transform struggling properties into thriving communities, develop future leaders, and create a lasting positive impact.

If there's one truth that stands above all others, it's this: Your success journey won't be a straight line—mine certainly hasn't been. But that's exactly as it should be. Progress isn't about perfection; it's about persistence. It's about getting up one more time than you fall down. And most importantly, it's about believing in yourself enough to keep going, even when others might doubt you.

You can't let the fear of failing stop you from taking action. I've faced plenty of moments where my confidence wavered, where the challenge seemed bigger than my abilities. But I've discovered that lacking confidence doesn't guarantee failure—it just means you're pushing your boundaries. Sometimes, you have to jump in and fake it until you make it. Each time you do, your real confidence grows a little stronger, and your capacity for success expands.

Success DNA, like our genetic code, provides the foundation. But it's our choices, our persistence, and our willingness to serve others that determine how that potential is expressed. In the end, success isn't about the big, dramatic moments—though they'll certainly come. It's about the small decisions we make every day, the consistent actions that align with our values, and the unwavering commitment to keep learning and growing, no matter how far we've come.

Decisions of Destiny:
Creating a Wave of Impact

Manuel R. Aragon

Manuel Aragon is a seasoned financial professional with a distinguished track record in tax preparation, accounting, and strategic finance. His expertise extends beyond conventional financial management, encompassing proactive cash planning and innovative tax strategies that drive tangible growth and operational efficiency. Across Colorado, Manuel has consistently delivered modern financial solutions, fostering a reputation for excellence and unparalleled client satisfaction.

His leadership is characterized by a client-centric approach, ensuring seamless onboarding and sustained positive relationships. Manuel's ability to translate complex financial concepts into actionable strategies has been instrumental in the success of numerous companies. He possesses a versatile skill set, demonstrated by his experience in diverse roles, including Tax Preparer, Chief Financial Officer, Operations Manager, Finance Director, and Consultant.

Manuel's comprehensive understanding of financial intricacies, coupled with his commitment to delivering tailored solutions, positions him as a trusted advisor and strategic partner. His dedication to staying abreast of evolving financial landscapes ensures that his clients benefit from the most current and effective financial practices.

https://www.facebook.com/profile.php?id=61564191257299

https://www.instagram.com/aragon_tax_return_services/

https://www.linkedin.com/company/aragon-tax-return-services

www.AragonTaxReturnServices.com

S uccess is a journey of gradually becoming a better version of yourself. It is a continuous process of self-improvement that extends beyond individual achievements—empowering others, especially younger family members like nieces and nephews and also my own son. Success means fostering a culture of empowerment that benefits everyone by teaching others to recognize their potential and take control of their lives.

Success Is Self-Improvement and Continuous Personal Growth

Achieving success requires commitment and sustained effort; it is a gradual process rather than an immediate result. Along the journey, obstacles often arise, leading to detours or setbacks. Therefore, it is crucial to remain connected to one's roots and core values. Staying true to these foundational principles enables me to realign with my ultimate goals, despite temporary deviations.

Personal growth demands patience and effort. As I grow older, what I once considered "mistakes" I now perceive as "decisions." Decisions—whether good or bad—are intricately intertwined with life and come with corresponding consequences or rewards. Equally important are mindset and self-reflection. Each day, I begin with the intention of improving by learning from past decisions and assessing how those choices have influenced my actions. This process allows me to consciously adjust my behavior, fostering more positive outcomes in the future.

Success is not defined by material wealth but by meaningful participation in activities that contribute to something greater than ourselves, such as inspiring future generations. These are essential elements of life that promote growth and evolution over time. This participation serves as a way to leave a lasting legacy. Ultimately, the overarching theme of success is self-improvement and continuous personal growth.

Significant Influences in My Life and Leadership Approach

One of the most significant influences in my life was my grandparents, particularly my grandmother. I lost her during my teenage years; she passed away about a month before I was transitioning out of a youth detention facility. The promise I made to her—to stay out of trouble and achieve academic success—became my guiding principle and served as the catalyst for a profound shift in my perspective and priorities. I returned to school a few years later, earned an associate's degree, and eventually launched my tax business the same year, fulfilling my promise while also demonstrating resilience, determination, and a strong commitment to personal growth.

Another important influence in my life was Dr. Gail Bailey, our church's pastor. She provided me with guidance and encouragement when

I was uncertain about my path in life. She urged me to return to school and recommended accounting classes, which became the foundation of my educational and professional journey. She shared advice, prayers, my first internship and book recommendations while consistently offering encouragement and direction.

A third key influence in my life was Erika Aragon, the mother of my son Xzander, who served as a steadfast support system. She stood by me as I balanced night school, full-time work, and the responsibilities of adult life in our first apartment. Her patience and unwavering support provided me with strength and stability during that period of personal growth and transition.

Most importantly, my faith in God serves as the cornerstone of my life and leadership approach, offering guidance and strength throughout my journey. Emerging from a challenging situation as a juvenile, the positive influences I encountered in both the church and workplace environments were invaluable. My mentors and support system not only provided guidance but also fostered an open and supportive atmosphere where I felt comfortable asking questions. Learning from experienced professionals, such as accountants, CPAs, and CFOs, who generously shared their knowledge and skills helped fill the gaps in my formal education. I also value the enduring relationships I've built with the companies I've been a part of.

Challenges in My Journey and Maintaining My Persistence

The greatest challenge I ever faced was being charged with a felony at the young age of 14 and enduring two years of isolation because of it. However, this experience became a pivotal moment for self-discovery and growth. It humbled me and revealed who my true friends, family, and support system were. It also taught me to move away from valuing material possessions and, instead, to focus on understanding my identity on a deeper level.

I confronted the obstacles head-on, including the stigma and barriers associated with having a criminal record. I worked twice as hard and studied twice as long to prove my capabilities, driven by a strong commitment to self-improvement. My resolve was truly tested when the IRS initially denied my application to become a tax preparer. In response, I wrote a heartfelt letter explaining my circumstances, upbringing, and the decisions that had led to my troubles. After several months of waiting, my application was finally approved. I refuse to let my past define me. Instead, I feel motivated and dedicated to becoming the best tax professional, CFO, Operations Manager, and leader I could be.

I start each year with clearly defined 30-day goals. Both short-term and long-term planning are crucial; therefore, I map out my objectives month by month to create a structured roadmap for achieving my aspirations. The tax season coincides with the first 120 days of the year and keeps us very busy, so I maintain a well-structured schedule to optimize productivity and stay on track with my goals. With an efficiency-oriented mindset, I strive to maximize my time and productivity by developing specific skills, such as using a 10-key calculator and multiple screens. These practices have enhanced my professional growth and reinforced my transparency with clients, showcasing my commitment to excellence. Additionally, my practice of prayer serves as a time for reflection, whether to seek guidance during difficulties or to express gratitude for life's blessings.

Being able to move away from the wrong path felt like a second chance from God, inspiring me during moments when I feel tired, overwhelmed, or busy during tax season. Moments of complacency can arise, and comfort with success can sometimes lead to mistakes. However, such missteps serve as valuable redirections, guiding me back onto a purposeful path.

I have been accustomed to hard work since a young age, with my father waking me up early to help deliver newspapers. This early experience continues to shape my approach to life. I have taken only six days off in 12 years, working from the road on countless family vacations, showcasing my relentless drive. I always strive to make the most of my time, whether through reading or engaging in other meaningful activities.

A Failure That Provided a Valuable Lesson

Around 2017–2018, I discovered an opportunity while working for a food production company, where I assisted with bookkeeping, cost modeling, and payroll, essentially my first startup business. Observing the company's challenges with sanitation and quality assurance needs, I took the initiative to address the issue creatively by launching M&M's Cleaning Services, named after my grandparents, Martha and Manuel. I provided a tailored solution to the company's sanitation needs and successfully ran the cleaning business for approximately 6 to 8 months.

Unfortunately, an accident occurred when one of the 200-gallon kettles snapped, spilling boiling water that caused injuries to my father, who was working for me at the time. It caused burns from his feet up to his knees, resulting in a drastic rise in my workers' compensation costs. Ultimately, these costs led to the closure of my company, marking my first business failure.

Nevertheless, I learned a valuable lesson about the critical importance of establishing a solid foundation and structure in business operations. Although costly, having insurance proved to be a lifesaving measure, shielding my father from severe financial and personal hardships during his recovery. Neglecting foundational elements when starting a business, however, can lead to significant challenges later. This incident became a transformative moment of growth, reinforcing the importance of patience, careful planning, and doing things properly from the very beginning.

Impact of Persistence on My Career and Personal Life

Persistence has been a transformative force in my life, enabling me to grow financially and, in turn, support my family, especially my closest family members. I have been fortunate to provide assistance to most in different circumstances, and that's something I am proud of. I've realized that I have a genuine passion for helping others. Thus, I became a community activist, leveraged my skills, and actively participated in church. Starting as a finance director at 18, I view my natural talents—logical thinking and problem-solving—as a skill set to positively impact others. My ability to inspire, teach, and coach those around me helped me foster growth, not just in myself but in the community as well.

My leadership approach is grounded in humility and patience, realizing that effective leadership requires time and understanding. Sharing my life story, including both my bad decisions and successes, can serve as a valuable lesson for others. Everyone's answers to life's questions are unique. By engaging in conversations and reflecting on how others view and approach challenges, we discover opportunities for mutual growth and learning.

I recommend learning from others' life stories and passing on lessons, particularly to the next generation. Looking at my now four-year-old son, I'm inspired to leave behind a legacy rooted in wisdom and understanding rather than ignorance, as I hope to guide him away from repeating my past mistakes.

Beyond personal goals, I also emphasize the broader responsibility of supporting others. Not everyone has access to strong support systems, mentors, or leaders, and I aspire to step into that role for those in need, bridging gaps and fostering growth in others. A key example of these positive influences is my emphasis on prayer, a meaningful and grounding practice I intend to carry forward.

Some lessons in life, however, can only be fully understood through personal experience. For instance, touching a hot stove despite warnings provides a direct experience that often leaves a more lasting impression than advice or guidance alone. Striking a balance between empathetic observation and first-hand experience is crucial, as both are essential.

Advice to Aspiring Leaders

Life's journey inevitably includes failures, setbacks, and moments of loss, and such experiences highlight the unpredictable and finite nature of life. This awareness inspires a sense of appreciation for the time we have and the connections we share with others, encouraging gratitude for the moments spent together. With regards to persistence, I advocate for adaptability. Achieving goals sometimes requires changing the approach rather than giving up, as flexibility and determination are essential for overcoming obstacles.

There's a distinction between a leader's and a follower's approach, and attitude often dictates results. A positive mindset leads to positive outcomes, while a negative mindset can bring setbacks. Mastering a positive mindset takes time and effort. I used to approach life with anger and frustration. Life felt overwhelming, but over time, I developed and mastered a more constructive mindset—one where challenges became opportunities for growth and improvement.

The decisions you make will inevitably impact others. Poor choices can result in "collateral damage" or unintended negative consequences. On the other hand, good decisions are like "seeds of growth," fostering positive outcomes over time. For instance, the choices I made in my late teens to pursue education and focus on personal development continue to yield benefits even 20-plus years later. Likewise, my past mistakes prompted necessary shifts in my mindset, leading to growth and maturity.

To the younger generation, my advice is to remain committed and driven. When you start school, you may not have everything figured out right away, but the decision to begin that journey is where true learning happens as you navigate the path.

Final Thoughts

I'm grateful for the opportunity to collaborate with other leaders, drawing inspiration from these experiences. Leadership is not an obligation but a choice—one that motivates me to stay on my path and strive for meaningful impact. I take pride in leaving a legacy for future generations, understanding the importance of creating a foundation that others can learn from. However, I am concerned about the potential decline of reading in an increasingly technology-driven world. Therefore, I aim to encourage the younger generation to embrace reading as a means of refining their skills and gaining valuable insights into how others navigate life's challenges.

Redefining Success: From Being a Self-Obsessed Narcissist to Becoming a Servant Leader

Maik Wiedenbach

Maik Wiedenbach is an award-winning fitness expert, elite coach, and former Olympic-level swimmer dedicated to transforming lives through strength training and nutrition. A two-time World Cup competitor for Germany, he earned degrees in history and German literature from Ruhr University Bochum and history and philosophy from Fordham University. After a successful career on Wall Street, Maik founded Maik Wiedenbach Personal Training NYC, now one of New York's top-rated gyms, with a second location in Dubai. Recognized as "Best Coach USA 2023," his expertise has been featured in Forbes, GQ, and Men's Health. As an educator at NYU, author, and sought-after speaker, Maik simplifies fitness, debunks industry myths, and helps high-achievers maximize results. His no-nonsense approach has made him a trusted authority for professionals, corporate travelers, and anyone seeking peak performance. Through his books, content, and training, he continues to redefine success in the fitness industry.

Success. That shiny prize we chase for decades—and hardly anyone catches. Writing this chapter made me realize how flawed our perception of success often is—and how much unhappiness its pursuit can create.

For some, success means Ferraris, Rolexes, or penthouses. For me, it used to mean beating the other guy—being the biggest in the room, making the most money, lifting the heaviest weights, training the most clients. Winning at all costs. But I've learned that real success has nothing to do with external validation. It's about internal alignment and contribution.

Keep in mind that I do believe in the free market and making money. But there's a point where the ROI starts to drop off. If you keep chasing society's definition of success, you will never truly feel successful. There will always be someone better, richer…fill in the blank.

This chapter is about that transformation—about crashing hard and rebuilding from rubble. From training clients 14 hours a day to building a brand that runs without me. From manic highs and hospital stays to therapy and facing old demons. From a one-man hustle to mentoring a team across continents.

If you're building something—anything—this chapter is for you. If you've ever hit a wall, questioned your sanity, or wondered if all the work means anything, you're in the right place. This isn't another chest-thumping entrepreneur memoir. It's real, ugly—but also kind of beautiful.

Success Principle #1: Evolve as a Leader

You can't lead until you've done the hard work of growing yourself first.

Just like my perception of success changed over the years, so did my leadership style, evolving from downright awful to (hopefully) better.

My first years of running my own business were marked by terrible leadership. I was an authoritarian; I mimicked the leaders I knew. I grew up in West Germany, where coaching was strictly top-down. The teacher, doctor, or coach was a demi-god; you were nobody. Naturally, I did the same.

If my employees didn't deliver, I'd ridicule them. I micromanaged every session they taught, thereby killing their confidence.

Unsurprisingly, my first employee stole from me—cash *and* clients! I brought him into the business—he was like a little brother! At first, I was furious about the betrayal. But eventually, I realized it was partly my fault.

I never gave him a clear roadmap to success, so he didn't feel any sense of loyalty.

That's when it hit me: **real leadership isn't about control—it's about setting people up for success.**

But I still didn't see the problem. It took a hard reset to become a better leader.

One of my darkest moments came in 2011. I found myself in a psych ward. Without diving into the details, I had an untreated manic episode (I'm bipolar 1) that caused very erratic behavior. I lost everything—my business was gone, I was temporarily separated from my wife, and the medication was making me unhealthy. My liver enzymes shot up, and my weight ballooned to 115 kilos—not muscle!

Things were bleak: a small bedroom, communal showers, and not much else.

Eventually, I stopped pitying myself and took control of what I could—my body. I had a friend bring me protein powder, oatmeal, and peanut butter. I started a prison-style workout: 2,000 push-ups, 1,000 squats, 1,000 lunges, and 1,000 crunches every day. (You have lots of time in a psych ward.)

That became the first step towards rebuilding my life.

Upon release, I entered a bodybuilding show…and won. Unreal!

For years, I was angry at the mental health system. But eventually, I realized that while the system is flawed, I also had to do my part. If I did not, I would end up dead within the year.

So I started therapy. Unpacked all my trauma. It was uncomfortable, brutal, but necessary.

Often, I wonder if that part of my life could've gone differently. But I know now: I had to go through it to get here.

Out of that failure and resurrection, I began to dial back my ego, and it finally led others.

But my growth as a leader wasn't finished.

Necessity made me the leader that I should've been during COVID.

In spring 2020, government orders shut down our gym, yet we still had to make money. At first, I couldn't pay my employees. I asked them to believe in my vision, to hold on through delayed payments. My solution? Offer affordable outdoor workouts, just enough to get our foot back in the door—then gradually raise prices as the economy recovered.

I learned a huge lesson: when people are actual business stakeholders, they perform better. Instead of micromanaging, I said, "You train in Central Park, you take the West Side, I'll handle downtown. We either pull this off and survive, or we go under." And it worked. We all took a massive (but temporary) pay cut, rallied as a group, and survived the biggest crisis New York had seen in a century.

With a second business in Dubai, I travel between two locations. The nine-hour time difference would make regular check-ins nearly impossible if I didn't trust my team to run things without me. They just get it done—because it's in their best interest too. When people are invested and believe in the vision, you get automatic buy-in. The business stops owning you—you start running it.

Lifting others up will ultimately make your life better.

What do I mean? Let me tell you about my protégé, Jay.

We met in 2020, when things didn't look great for him. He was in dire straits. But he grew on me; I really liked his personality. Over the months that followed, he shadowed me around the gym like a puppy—eager to learn about training and nutrition.

At some point, I said, "You like training, you're good with people—why not get paid for it? Get certified and join us."

From there, there was no stopping Jay. He worked non-stop. In addition to building his six-figure business, he also became leaner, dropping about 80 pounds over 18 months. I pushed him to take it further, got him a professional photoshoot, and helped capture a fantastic before-and-after. Along the way, we built a deep friendship.

Fast forward to 2022, I won "Best Personal Trainer USA" from *Men's Journal*, a huge moment for me and my team. Part of that honor? A billboard in Times Square! We chose Jay's before-and-after since it was so dramatic and powerful. On a warm August night, we gathered—me, the team, Jay, even his mom—right in the middle of Times Square to see him up in lights. My goosebumps had goosebumps!

That is the ultimate success story—a mentor and mentee working together to create the greater good.

Success Principle #2: The Market Is Always Right

Never be afraid to pivot.

The persistence that got me through my mental health crisis proved vital in navigating unpredictable business environments.

When uncertainty hits, my initial reaction is frustration. Sometimes, even anger. I usually spend two or three days venting, fuming about how unfair everything is.

But after that, I ask myself, "Ok, now what do I do?" I remind myself: I cannot influence global politics, but I can protect my inner circle.

Take the 2008 financial crisis as an example. It hit New York hard—roughly 400,000 jobs in the city depended on the financial industry. On a personal level, things were tense. My wife was in grad school, so my tiny, just-launched business was our only source of income.

With mostly Wall Street clients, I worried personal training wouldn't survive a crisis. Surprisingly, the opposite happened. The stress made my clients more focused on their health. Suddenly, wellness wasn't optional. They started coming more often.

One of my clients was the Chief of Staff at the New York Federal Reserve. With him clocking 100-hour weeks, he couldn't come to the gym. So I went to him. Soon, I led small group classes in the war rooms of AIG, Merrill Lynch, and Bank of America. I'd show up with bands and protein bars, running 20-minute sessions to help clear their heads.

Yes, the situation was scary. But it taught me: you can't control the world—only how you respond.

Success Principle #3: Play the Long Game *and* Dominate Your Niche

Want lasting success? Play the long game—think in decades, not months or years.

If you bought a basketball today, your NBA debut is at least a decade away… if you make it at all. The same applies to starting a business: the chances are slim, and the path is long and grueling.

If you want to be an entrepreneur, forget about making money for the first decade. Seriously. You'll reinvest most of your income. Success follows a hockey stick pattern—flatlining while your peers get promotions and raises. Stick with it, work seven days a week, and you *might* see the payoff in 10 years. If that doesn't excite you, entrepreneurship might not be your path.

But patience alone isn't enough—you need focus too. You need to dominate your niche.

At my gym, every machine is custom-made for maximum muscle tension. Our focus? Fat loss and muscle gain. We don't do treadmills. We don't offer cardio, rehab, or Pilates. If people want to get bigger or leaner, we're their spot. If not, no hard feelings.

Jim Collins calls this the Hedgehog Concept: find your edge and stay sharp.

A hedgehog has one strategy: it rolls into a ball so it can't be eaten. That's it. But it works.

Success Principle #4: Vision Is Great, Habits Get You There

Vision gets you out of bed—and through the grueling, often unpaid hours of startup life.

However, many entrepreneurs focus too much on their vision and not enough on the steps to get there. Yes, you need to see the horizon—but you also need to crush the daily tasks that move you forward. Without that, a vision remains a pipe dream.

"So, is this where motivation comes in?"

Not really. Motivation is overrated. Motivation gets you through a tough day, but it eventually fades.

So, how does one stay the course when things get difficult? You build habits. Daily, non-negotiable ones.

When preparing for the Nationals and the World Cups, I trained three times a day, five to six hours total. Nobody wakes up thinking, "I can't wait to do that." You just do it because it's what you do.

My vision is to build a world-class personal training empire—with exclusive gyms in the most desirable cities on the planet. New York. Dubai. Singapore. Abu Dhabi. LA. I want clients to walk into any of our locations, pull up their personalized workout, and have a trainer ready to execute with precision. Think: the Four Seasons of fitness—cutting-edge equipment, top-tier service, and consistent excellence.

Remember Jay from earlier? *That's* the transformation I am looking for!

To make that happen, I put in the work every day: generating new clients, growing my team, creating content, shooting videos, and making sure existing clients are progressing.

There's no epiphany—just persistence.

The Highs, the Lows, and the Lessons Between

I'm grateful for the past three decades. Nearing 50, I feel like I've lived four lives—filled with highs and lows, set against the backdrop of a fascinating city.

I've competed at the World Cup—and locked in a psych ward.

I've graced a bodybuilding magazine cover—and gone bankrupt three times.

If my experiences help you dodge a few mistakes, that's a win.

You don't need to be perfect to build something great.

You don't need a clean past or a polished pitch.

You need grit, clarity, and a bias for action.

Running your own company isn't for the faint of heart. There will be sleepless nights, wondering if you'll make payroll or cover rent. No mothership's coming to save you. It's your life, your team's lives, and their families too. Think hard: do you want that responsibility?

My career? It's like the Amazon River—twisting and turning. I've been named Best Coach, faced epic failures, and experienced everything in between.

Would I do it all over again? Absolutely.

Entrepreneurship isn't for everyone. Only do it if you value freedom over safety.

If that's you, rock on.

Viel Glück!

PART III

Achieving Success

Always the Next Summit

Dr. Javier Cavada

*Dr. Javier Cavada is a global energy leader and industrial engineer specializing in **energy transition and sustainable innovation**. As **President and CEO of Mitsubishi Power** for **Europe, the Middle East, and Africa**, he drives the transformation of energy systems across three continents. With over two decades in executive leadership—including 17 years at Wärtsilä, where he led global energy operations in 170 countries—Javier brings deep expertise in technology, resilience, and strategic growth.*

*Today, alongside his executive role at Mitsubishi, he is also the **owner of JC Navalips** with several manufacturing locations—including the factory where he started his career at Wärtsilä—as well as a **Board Member at Galp**, the Portuguese energy multinational.*

*He holds a **PhD in Industrial Engineering**, an **MBA**, and a **degree in Psychology**, and has been honored as **Distinguished Alumnus** by both the **University of Cantabria** and the **University of Liverpool**. A recipient of the **2024 Blue Industry Award of Cantabria**, Javier chairs several influential organizations in the energy sector, including **Gazelle Wind** and **EU Turbines**.*

*Having lived in **China** for many years and led businesses across **the Americas, Europe and Australia**, Javier shares his vision for a future powered by **persistence, innovation, and purpose-driven leadership**.*

Success Is a Moving Target

I define success as a deep sense of fulfillment and accomplishment more than just the end of a journey. Success for me is about overcoming challenges, making an impact, and leaving something behind that inspires others. Success includes the fight, the failures, the lessons, and then building a legacy from it all. Without failure, success doesn't mean anything. Like pleasure without pain, it's the Yin and the Yang.

I strive for it every morning, every evening, every month. I don't say, "What's success?" I ask, "What's my target?" I build ladders toward it, including ambitious targets, and then programs, steps, and stages. If it all goes according to plan, it's science fiction. That's not real life. You need setbacks. You need surprises. And they will come, even if you do not wish for it.

I've always felt extremely lucky, having been way more successful than I could have ever imagined. But each achievement becomes the basement for the next. In 2013, just back from China, I fought like a bull for a Global VP role, leading thousands across two continents. Then, I got it. They said I was young, unexpected, and maybe it was even too soon. They were probably right. But that was the launchpad. And I said, "Now I'll make others successful. I'll make the people who believed in me proud." That, to me, is what success is. And then, when you get 6 out of 10, you fight for more. That's the game. Keep aiming higher. Always.

Success Evolves with Every Step

Success has definitely evolved for me. I remember being around 28 years old, sitting in a leadership training session, in the middle of a forest in the Netherlands. At that time, I was managing a few hundred people. A consultant asked, "Who wants to be the next CEO?" and I just stayed silent. What did it even mean to be a CEO? I had no clue. Back then, success for me was simple: I wanted to have a life as accomplished as my father's. That was my goal.

Then, when I was 25, I realized, "Damn, I have already achieved what I was planning to." And suddenly, I found myself thinking, "Now what? Do I just survive until retirement in this role? Forty years doing the same?" That was when my mindset shifted. I started asking, "Could I fight for my boss's role? Maybe in ten years?" But ten years felt too long. It wasn't about climbing anymore, but rather, it was about proving what was possible.

Now, I tell my daughter something I've come to live by: Make life memorable. Squeeze every bit out of it. If I can achieve what someone considers a lifetime of success in just three years, then that's really good. Then, I go for the next one. Every three years, I find myself in places I didn't even know existed. For me, it's about discovering and knowing there's always more to come.

Shaped by Leadership—The Good and the Bad

Just as failures teach you more than successes, leadership is shaped by both positive and negative experiences. In fact, toxic leaders can teach you some of the most valuable lessons about how to become an outstanding leader, though oftentimes painfully.

I have had great mentors who left a lasting impact, but I have also encountered arrogance, disrespect, and leaders who simply could not fill the shoes they were wearing. These experiences pushed me to strive for better leadership, using "the other type" of leaders as examples of what not to be.

One of the most pivotal moments in my leadership journey came when I moved from a blue-chip German automotive company to a much smaller firm, stepping into a general manager role at just 26 years old. The level of opposition, plots, and dirty tricks I encountered made me want to quit—on my second day, my third day, and my fourth day. But I chose to fight. That decision built my resilience, strengthened my positivity, and gave me the mental fortitude that defines my leadership today.

Failure as Fuel for Leadership

Failure is an inevitable part of any leadership journey. I truly believe that you can never reach your maximum performance levels without experiencing failure from different angles and at high intensity. It's like in sports—the most successful leaders must go through the toughest situations to bring their teams to peak performance. If you haven't failed, maybe you haven't tried hard enough or taken the most demanding path.

One of the most painful failures I've experienced was when I built a compelling business plan for market expansion—strong numbers, solid strategy, small investment—and still couldn't get full approval from the board. A couple of years later, it was clear: we should have gone all in. But success—rising share prices, top market position—created risk aversion. I've been told, "Javier, we love what you do, but we don't want to destroy the company by expanding too fast." That stays with me.

When things don't go as planned, when your most obvious next move is blocked, it becomes a personal pain trip. I've had this happen in multiple organizations—when you reach a certain level, others around you start saying, "Let's just keep it like this; it's unnecessary to push further." I take that as a failure to be convincing and achieve.

But I don't dwell. I extract the lesson, and I fight again. From the toughest times, I've gained the power to keep going. The good moments? I celebrate quickly, then move on because there's always a new level waiting to be reached.

Speed, Simplicity, and Handling Uncertainty

When I think about growth, I don't just mean revenue or profit, which, of course, are important. For me, real growth is about people: my team. But to achieve that, you need movement. Growth doesn't happen in stillness. You need to accelerate the movement and get the energy going. In many organizations, complexity, rules, and fear slow everything down. People are running, yes, but like a mouse on a wheel. It takes lots of effort but offers no direction.

That's why I always talk about speed and simplicity. You need both. Speed alone doesn't help if there's no traction or if you're just spinning. Simplicity removes traps, removes unnecessary bureaucracy, and clears the mental barriers that keep teams from evolving. I've seen it in large organizations, whether in Japan, the US or the UK, and everywhere, it is the same—"We've always done it this way," or "It's too risky." But when you simplify, remove silos, and let people run on flat ground, you get real progress.

I've always avoided the 9-to-5, stay-in-your-lane nightmare. It's not just boring, but it's also a trap. So I handle uncertainty by pushing for clarity, for motion, and for freeing people to do meaningful work without the weight of complexity slowing them down. That's how you create the space for real growth.

From Setback to Breakthrough in China

One of the biggest challenges I've faced—and one that shaped me deeply—was when I moved to China between 2008 and 2013. I had been leading operations in Europe and was asked to boost our growing business in the Far East—bringing in technology and transferring know-how. When I first arrived, everything seemed to be working well. The mission was clear: expand and develop. But just days after starting, the truth surfaced: things were not running well at all.

We had serious technical issues, supply chain problems, and people challenges. On top of that, our headquarters had decided to shut down a large part of manufacturing in Europe and move these operations to China. So, what started as a growth assignment quickly became a complete transformation project. Suddenly, I was tasked with building factories, relocating people, leading knowledge transfers, everything.

It could've been a nightmare, and at moments, it felt like one. But looking back, it was a dream assignment. I had to stretch beyond my limits, stay positive, use a bit of black humor, and push forward with persistence. I grew up in those years. I became a different leader and a transformational one.

That experience also increased my love for growth, change, and dynamism. It also gave me my leadership motto: speed and simplicity.

Staying the Course with Calm and Flexibility

Maintaining persistence requires mental strength, peace of mind, and intentional strategies. My wife often says, "In case of nuclear war or natural disaster, look at Javier—he will remain calm and plan the best way forward without a drop of sweat." She surely exaggerates, but life has taught me that panicking takes you nowhere. When facing adversity, I believe in reframing challenges as opportunities. There's only one situation you can't resolve— and that's death. From everything else, you can extract growth, innovation, or at least a lesson.

Persistence is also about knowing you don't have to do everything alone. None of us are superheroes in the Marvel sense. The key to success is people—building a support network over time with a strong commitment. Surrounding yourself with mentors, peers, and advisors is essential. They bring fresh insights and, more importantly, motivation when times are tough.

Above all, persistence isn't just about being consistent but being flexible. You will never reach a relevant target in a straight line. It's about adapting, knowing when to pivot, and understanding that sometimes sticking to a failing strategy isn't persistence but more of a lack of adaptability. The journey to success is full of twists, and great things are never easy. But shared achievements, born from these moments, are worth much more.

I've joked with my wife many times, "Come on, I could retire already." But deep down, I know that would be a horrible life for me. Sure, I've thought about it, but it just doesn't make any sense. I'm not built for repetition or comfort zones. I need a challenge. I need complexity. I need to grow.

As I approach 50, I know I could choose to just enjoy, but that would feel like giving up. It would be, honestly, a suicidal move. I need to keep my mind dynamic, my goals evolving, and my journey forward. That's what drives me.

Merging Mission with Meaning

Balancing leadership and personal life is one of the greatest challenges any leader faces. But rather than striving for a perfect 50/50 split, I believe we have a mission in life: a purpose that integrates both personal and professional goals. They are not separate worlds but interconnected. As I always tell my teenage daughter, she is the most important business I have to run. If I fail at home, I can't truly succeed anywhere else.

To make this work, it's essential not to walk the leadership journey alone. Having the right life partner and a strong support network is crucial. Delegation also plays a huge role. It's crucial to trust your team rather than trying to control every detail. That's how effective leadership is sustained.

And then there's downtime where you intentionally carve out moments to recharge. Whether it's reading, relaxing on the couch, working out, or mindfulness practices, these are not luxuries but necessities. Your hobbies are your charging station. Without them, high performance is unsustainable.

I know that when I walk into a board meeting, some may think, "Here he comes again." Yes, I come with ambition, with the drive for more, for better. Because that's who I am. I'm committed to speed, simplicity, and meaningful, sustainable success.

Make It Memorable

If I had one piece of advice to give on persistence, it would be this: strive for a meaningful life, not just an existence. Too many people pass through the decades without building memories that matter. I always tell aspiring leaders and even my daughter that you must create a life filled with landmark moments. Every ten years, something should stand out. A purpose. An achievement. A legacy.

In life, it's important not just to work hard but to keep on doing better: being more educated, wiser, more generous, and more impactful. Let people talk about you with a smile. Let them say, "He made things better." That's real success.

Vision Rooted in Legacy, Fueled by Ambition

Since 2021, I've had a very clear vision. It was somewhat bold, even ambitious. I already own my industrial company, and we are acquiring others. My dream is to grow this into a business large enough to rival the global brands I've worked for. I want to become the proud CEO of that company, one strong enough to compete on the world stage.

But even more important, I want my 17-year-old daughter to one day take over. It has to be her choice, and so far, it is. She's preparing to start university soon and is also starting to focus on business. I want to build something lasting, something that passes from generation to generation, like the founder of Banco Santander from my hometown, whose granddaughter now runs one of the world's biggest banks. I want to leave that kind of legacy. Too ambitious? Maybe. But that makes it a meaningful goal.

I've already achieved far more than I ever imagined. Still, I keep going—active at 1 a.m., rising again at 6 a.m.—because I want to achieve even more. Growing a great organization, making it larger, happier and more successful, is an incredibly inspiring journey. Politics? Tempting, but I'm not interested. Too much dirt and mediocrity. But who knows—I'm still only 49.

From No Clue to Clarity: The Shift from 30-Year-Old Javier to Now

At 30, I had no clue about long-term implications. I was more relaxed about my legacy, careless with my habits, sleeping less, drinking more, and eating unhealthy food. I looked good, but treated myself badly. Today, at 49, I'm much healthier and more conscious. For me, living to 100 only matters if you live well.

Back then, I was a managing director in Spain, had a lovely wife and a newborn daughter, and taught university classes at night. I had ticked all the boxes: career, family, recognition. But deep down, I was thinking: "Now what? Just keep going for 35 years until retirement?" That sounded horrific.

Then, an opportunity came to go to China. Most of my friends thought I had gone mad, leaving everything behind. But for me, it was like a Christopher Columbus moment. No one I knew had done it, but I thought, "If I don't try, I'll regret it." That move changed my life. I went from climbing the ladder I could see to realizing there was a whole galaxy beyond Mount Olympus.

Now, I ask myself: "What's next?" It has to be tougher, more meaningful, and even more exciting.

Three Things I Want My Daughter to Always Remember

If I had to write just a few things on a whiteboard for my daughter to carry with her through life, here's what they would be.

First—**Don't let anyone limit you.** Most of the world is trying to place limits on others—on what you can do and what you can become. Society, culture, and even friends sometimes do it. Every time someone achieves something extraordinary, people say it was luck or genius. But it's not. It's usually someone with drive who refuses to be boxed in. So don't let anyone put a ceiling on you—not even yourself.

Second—**Trust**. Trust yourself. And trust your parents. We may not fully understand what you're capable of, but we'll always be your biggest cheerleaders. No one will ever be prouder of your journey than us—even when it gets hard or complicated.

Third—**Choose the right partner.** This isn't business advice—it's about life. The person beside you can be your greatest accelerator or your biggest weight. Through life, I have realized how much my wife grounds me. She helps me stay connected to my roots. That kind of person is rare and priceless. Choose wisely.

Talking about choosing a partner, I was very fortunate to find my wife. Back then, we were both on our late twenties and knew we wanted to be together. We moved in, got married few years later, and had our amazing daughter the next year. It felt like a Hollywood script: everything was smooth, everything easy. At that point, I thought, "Okay, we'll have three kids and live a normal life." But then came China.

I went first to see if it would work. After six months, I told her, "It's not good—it's amazing." She joined me with our one-year-old daughter. Two days in, she was so unhappy. It was too much. It was too different, overwhelmingly different. So, she went back to Spain.

For five years, we lived apart. I commuted every two months, she visited in summer, our daughter came for a few months every year. It wasn't the plan, but she became a rock. My rock. I'm always sailing—she's the port I return to. If your home life isn't solid, everything collapses. She didn't sign up for this life, but she gave me the stability to lead.

In hindsight, I couldn't have done any of it without her. Many options could've ended badly, but she made the impossible work. That's what made her the one.

After years spent in the Far East without my family, the next chapters took us across Europe, together. My daughter has grown up with a front-row seat to the vastness of the world—and she has embraced it. From two years in Trieste to three years in Helsinki, to the last seven in London, she has lived across cultures, learned from diversity, and blossomed into a global citizen. Now, as she completes her International Baccalaureate and enters a top global university, she is more prepared for a rich, fulfilling life of purpose, growth, and wonder than I ever was at her age. That, to me, is legacy: not just what you achieve, but what you pass on.

In parallel, my own fuel—the drive that keeps me pushing, leading, evolving—is no longer about personal ambition. It's about helping others rise. True success is never a solo act. It's about lifting your circle, elevating those around you, and making your shared world better. That's the kind of success worth living—and leading—for.

Guided by Intuition

Dr. Glen N. Robison

Dr. Glen Robison serves as a Diplomate of the American Board of Multiple Specialties in Podiatry. He's board certified in Primary Care in Podiatric Medicine. He is also a Jin Shin Jyutsu practitioner and certified Myopractor, trained in releasing deep restrictions of motion in the body that reside at the root of our symptoms and ailments.

His works include Amazon Bestseller: Healthy Dad Sick Dad: "What Good Is Your Wealth If You Don't Have Your Health?" and USA Today Bestseller Anthology Book: Luminary Leadership "How top Entrepreneurs lead in business and in life." He is inducted into the prestigious Marquis Who's Who.

Dr. Robison leads his medical specialty in the use of Prolotherapy for stabilizing ankles, repairing torn ligaments and tendons, along with reducing bunions without surgery. He was a part of a medical mission to the Kingdom of Tonga.

Dr. Robison currently operates his private practice of twenty-five years in Mesa, Arizona, where he provides necessary services to his patients, both surgically and clinically. When not in clinic or writing books, he spends time studying and perfecting the Master of Art in oil painting and playing with his dog.

https://www.drglenrobison.com/

My biggest challenge wasn't a single moment—it was a recurring battle with standardized tests. It started with the American College Test (ACT) in high school. The ACT is a standardized exam used for college admissions in the United States, evaluating a student's preparedness for college by measuring their abilities in key academic areas. I saw tests as a pass-or-fail gateway: succeed and move forward, fail and fall behind. That belief weighed on me, especially after scoring a seven on the ACT. Looking back, it's almost surreal that someone with that score made it into college, let alone became a surgeon.

In medical school, I realized I was a visual learner but that didn't make test-taking easier. Watching students finish early broke also my focus. That's when I learned the power of tunnel vision—blocking out distractions, sitting at the front, and training myself to get to answers faster.

The real test came with the national boards. I failed by one percentage point—four times. For three years, I kept going. On my final attempt, with only one chance left, I scored 90%. Persistence and tunnel vision got me through—and changed my life.

The Guiding Light of Adversity

As a kid, I loved sports, but sports didn't always love me back. I developed asthma, likely triggered by childhood vaccinations, and it kept me from playing the games I enjoyed. At ten years old, I refused to accept that fate and set out on a mission to find a cure for my asthma.

I experimented on myself, forcing asthma attacks by running or biking and tracking how long it took for them to happen. I documented everything—what I ate, how long I exercised, and what triggered my symptoms. In college, I even worked with an allergist, thinking I'd go into that field. But something didn't feel right.

We often see setbacks as failures, but I believe they are valuable. When we keep our goal in mind and follow intuition over personal will—what I call reasoning—we reach our destination in ways we never expected.

Adversity is not a stumbling block but a guiding light. Challenges may make us feel lost, but they keep us aligned with where we are meant to be. God sees the path even when we can't. If we trust in that process, we will always end up exactly where we need to be.

Balancing Leadership and Personal Life

There's a best-selling book that I wrote called *Healthy Dad Sick Dad*, with a chapter called Yin Yang. A lot of people have trouble with that chapter, but it's very simple—it's about balance. In life, just like in health, balance is everything. When I talk to people about their health, I tell them to pay attention to how they feel. I even eat based on my body temperature. It may sound odd, but your body functions best at 98.6 degrees Fahrenheit. Drop below that, and you're more susceptible to illness. Balance matters in food, in health, and in life.

Leadership and personal life work the same way. When I walk into a room at work, I never know what I'm going to face. When I'm in surgery, I am laser-focused—no distractions, no background noise. My only goal is to get my patient better. But once I leave that space, I switch gears.

Too many people bring their work stress home. They get so caught up in their jobs that they forget to enjoy life. Balance means knowing when to shut work off. It means truly being present in each moment. Work is work, and personal life is personal. Both deserve your full attention—but at the right time.

Redefining Failure: A Mind Exercise

Failure, disappointment, and trials are not setbacks—they are mind exercises. Just as the body needs physical exercise to grow stronger, the mind needs challenges to develop. People often fixate on failure, but I believe the greatest successes come directly from what others might call failures.

In high school, I scored a seven on the ACT—not exactly a score that opens doors. I could have let that define me, but every challenge pushed me in the right direction. That's why we don't just accept failures but celebrate them. They are signposts showing we are on the right path. Instead of seeing failures as roadblocks, see them as opportunities. Reframing failure as a mind exercise turns fear into curiosity. Failure wasn't the end—it was the way forward.

The Power of Persistence

Persistence has played a critical role in both my career and personal life, but I've learned that persistence is also about who you surround yourself with. It's so important to gravitate toward people with the same mindset, people who are positive and driven. In life, you'll encounter what I call the "leeches"—negative people who thrive on pulling others down. They don't want to see your progress because they're stuck in their own misery, and their greatest challenge is trying to make you just as miserable.

But if you stay in tune, you'll also recognize the right individuals—the ones placed in your life to help guide you forward. And when you find them, hold on to them. For me, my wife is my number one supporter. She is the one who helps me through challenges, keeps me focused, and pushes me toward my goals.

Surround yourself with people who believe in you, who challenge you, and who push you forward. They will be the ones who help you turn persistence into progress.

Navigating Uncertainty: Trusting a Higher Source

I remember a lady coming into my office with a swollen toe. The MRI showed an infection, and they wanted to know if I needed to amputate. As I examined her, something didn't feel right. The X-ray and MRI pointed to infection, but my intuition said otherwise. I asked her, "Do you want your toe amputated?" She said, "No, if you can save it, let's save it." So, I told her, "I want to try something."

I scheduled surgery, planning to take a bone sample. But when I arrived, the biopsy kit wasn't there. They asked if I wanted to reschedule, but I refused. Instead, I asked for the smallest drill bit they had. In my mind, I had already visualized the procedure—drilling a small hole, collecting bone dust, and sending it for testing.

Just before making the incision, I set aside everything I had been taught and said a prayer. When I drilled the hole, something incredible happened—a tiny black cactus popped out of the bone. That was the cause of her infection. Had I been off by even a millimeter, I never would have found it. I removed the cactus and cleaned the area, and she never needed the amputation.

Uncertainty is inevitable. But in moments like this, I rely on a higher source beyond my own skills.

Mastering Persistence and Achieving Success

I follow three simple principles given to me by an orthopedic doctor: availability, affability, and ability. Patients need to feel heard and understood. Your skills and talents come last—people may have heard of your abilities, but until they meet you, it's your availability and affability that matter most.

In life, I also see success through three other key factors: prayer, faith, and visualization. Prayer is communication with God, and His way of responding is through intuition—gut feelings, hunches, or signs. Faith is about seeing success as if it's already achieved. When you give thanks for something as if you've already received it, it changes everything. I also see life as a canvas. Every painting starts with unseen layers, just like success. Every mistake and every lesson is embedded in your journey. Others will only see the finished product, but you must appreciate every stroke that led you there.

A Lesson for Future Leaders

The most important thing you can do for success is to help others succeed. Ask yourself—are you leading to control, or to uplift those around you? Success also starts with self-love. To truly love and uplift others, you must first love yourself. When you understand your true potential, you'll want to help others reach theirs, too. Don't be stingy with your talents—give freely, and success will come back to you.

The Value of Mentorship and Support

People need mentors. Yes, we have God in our lives, but He often places mentors along our journey to guide us. One of the most valuable mentors in my life was the *Healthy Dad*, whom I wrote about in my book. When my daughter was two and a half, she suddenly couldn't eat. I took her to pediatricians, and tried everything Western medicine had to offer—nothing worked. Frustrated, I called my mentor. He simply said, "Bring her down." Within minutes of adjusting her mid-back, she sat up and said, "Daddy, I'm hungry." She never had the problem again.

At that moment, I knew I had to learn from him. I spent years studying his techniques, and today, I use them in my practice to help patients who've suffered for years. Another mentor in my life is my art instructor. Every Wednesday, we sit down and paint, and I traded my scalpel for a paintbrush. My goal? To paint a Mona Lisa that will one day be remembered and placed in an art gallery.

Staying Motivated: The Power of Midway Goals

Having a long-term goal is valuable, but midway goals are just as important. When my high school counselor told me I wouldn't make it to college, I set my goal: First, get into college. Then, I finished college, became a surgeon, and then treated patients in Tonga—this last one was not even on my radar yet. Even though my ultimate goal was to become a surgeon, it took many steps to get there, which were my midway goals. When I accomplished my long-term goal, I set another long-term goal with multiple midway points. This is the process I use in life.

After earning my associate's degree, I stayed focused, even when distractions could have pulled me away. Always keep your long-term goal in mind and use your midway goals to keep you focused.

Success is a lifelong journey. Each milestone leads to the next. Once you reach your goal, don't stop—keep setting new ones. Stay focused, embrace each step, and always push forward.

The Vision That Keeps Me Going

There's a poem that has helped me in life once. My mom sent me *Don't Quit* by Edgar A. Guest. "When things go wrong as they sometimes will, When the road you're trudging seems all uphill…Rest if you must, but don't you quit. Success is failure turned inside out…It may be near when it seems afar, So, stick to the fight when you're hardest hit—It's when things go wrong that you mustn't quit."

When I was frustrated—and believe me, there were many times this happened—I would refer to this poem, and it would help put my mind back on track. So many people quit when success is just days away. One more step, one more effort—you could be right at the breakthrough.

Had I given up after failing my first physiology test in medical school, I would have never become a surgeon, and never saved lives. Persistence matters. I may never know the full impact of my work, but my mission is simple: never quit, always serve.

The Power of Promises and Persistence

Personal growth, for me, is deeply tied to the promises I've made. One of the most profound experiences in my life was my death experience during medical school. After suffering a severe anaphylactic reaction, the doctor's report stated it took them four hours to resuscitate me. On the other side, I made a choice—I had promised my brother I'd attend his wedding, and that promise was so binding that I asked to come back.

Another promise I made was to my Tongan friend in college. He helped me through physics and math, and I vowed that if I ever became a doctor, I'd go to Tonga and treat his people. Eleven years later, I fulfilled that promise.

Promises are powerful. They are more than words; they set a course in the universe. Outside of my professional life, these commitments have shaped me, reminding me that integrity and persistence lead to incredible life-changing results.

Final Thoughts: Life Is a Boomerang

Life is not difficult—we just make it difficult. What we put out into the world, we receive in return. If we carry anger, frustration, or guilt, we will attract the same. But if we radiate love, kindness, and joy, that's what will surround us. Life is a boomerang.

True success comes from lifting others up. When we serve others, we serve God, and in doing so, we unlock our true potential—our spiritual DNA. Trials, failures, and setbacks are just mental exercises, shaping us for greater success. No great achievement comes without them. Shift your mindset. See challenges as stepping stones, not roadblocks. If you do, life will open up in ways you never imagined. Your future is bright—embrace it.

Crisis Management and Handling Risks

Jochen Schwenk

As CEO of Crisis Control Solutions LLC, based in Naples, Florida, and Schwenk AG, headquartered in Zurich, Switzerland, Jochen Schwenk is a trailblazer in risk mitigation and crisis management. Widely regarded as a leading authority in his field, Jochen's expertise is sought after by governments, industries, and Fortune 500 companies. His clients include some of the world's most prestigious car manufacturers, such as Audi, Lamborghini, Porsche, and Volkswagen.

A distinguished author and founding member of Harvard's Presidents Circle, Jochen is also a member of other prestigious organizations, including the Forbes Council and Harvard Square. His deep understanding of complex challenges stems from an extensive background in military and intelligence operations—details of which remain deliberately discreet—adding a unique edge to his approach to risk and crisis management.

Together with his team of passionate and highly skilled professionals, Jochen has developed industry-defining strategies, particularly in addressing critical supply chain issues that impact global markets. His firm's services span a wide spectrum, from geopolitical consulting to proactive solutions for industrial disruptions, always staying ahead of the curve to deliver unparalleled value to clients.

Under Jochen's visionary leadership, Crisis Control Solutions and Schwenk AG have set the gold standard in crisis preparedness and resolution, empowering organizations to face the unthinkable with confidence and resilience.

Donald Rumsfeld, who served as Secretary of Defense under two US presidents, Gerald Ford and George W. Bush, has a famous quotation that explains why there is always uncertainty that people will encounter in life, whether in business or in their personal lives. He said, "There are known knowns—things we know we know. There are known unknowns—things we know we don't know. But there are also unknown unknowns—things we don't know we don't know." Thus, a lot of things can happen that can ruin a plan and cause a crisis situation.

As we go about our business and personal lives, we are always faced with risks and uncertainty, and even the best plans can get waylaid if we are not ready for the disappointments that come our way. That is why most companies need to have someone who usually has a team to handle risks and manage crises.

In this chapter, I will be emphasizing the importance of persistence in achieving success, whether in business or personal life. I have personally experienced how persistence has helped me gain the trust of Fortune 500 companies, making me their go-to risk and crisis manager. In my personal life, persistence has helped me get published in renowned platforms like Forbes, and I now contribute to bestselling books while at the same time balancing family and personal growth. I can truly say that these opportunities would not have existed without the strong determination to push through despite early rejections and challenges.

Can We Prepare for Those Unexpected Disappointments?

Yes, it is possible to prepare yourself for sudden, unexpected problems resulting from uncertainties and unknowns that can affect the business. Preparation is crucial, and it served me well when I was in the military and now in business and my personal life. Serving in the Armed Forces has given me the useful habit of anticipating worst-case scenarios and developing contingencies. This is known as contingency planning and is a vital process for anyone or any company to at least minimize the negative impact of disruptions and unforeseen events. This can save the company's reputation by minimizing the damages and allowing the business to recover from any setback in much less time than without planning and preparation.

My job as a leader is to be flexible and readily adapt to whatever situation we are faced with. And it is vital to provide the team with the right tools to get them prepared and be tough and resilient when the going gets tough. We just need to be persistent in working towards our goals, even in the face of adversity.

How to Handle Failure

Failure is a part of life. Obviously, nobody wants to fail, but sooner or later, you will come face to face with failure. What separates true leaders from those who are not is their attitude toward failure and how they handle it. In fact, I often encounter these situations quite frequently. And my job as a leader is to motivate my team to find a solution. In fact, you have to continuously develop solutions all day long. After the failure has been resolved, I analyze with my team what went wrong, and if a mistake was made on our part, we discuss and plan on how to avoid making the same mistake again in the future.

I always remind myself and my team that failure is a teacher, and it is not the final result. This is why persistence is crucial. And it is important to remember that Rome was not built in a day. When the problem is a very tough one, what you need to do is divide it into smaller, more manageable sizes and focus on the resolution of each of these bite-sized problems until the whole problem is finally resolved. Always remember—you need to be tough and always adaptable and flexible.

That is why it is vital to have a mentor and support system. My mentor has been one of my most important instructors in military and intelligence. He is more than fifteen years older than I am, and he continues to be my best friend. I am very grateful that I met him because having him as a mentor was life-changing for me. He taught me the power of leading from behind—allowing others to shine and providing strategic guidance while in the background. This particular philosophy has enabled me to lead more effectively in high-stakes corporate situations, allowing my teams to function at their highest potential.

Habits and Strategies That Can Help

When I served, I learned about strategies and habits we can develop to keep us persistent and resilient in the face of challenges and obstacles. Being always prepared for the unexpected is crucial, and it works just as well in business as in personal life. I have developed the habit of thinking about all the possible events that may happen and always thinking in scenarios. This way, my team and I will be prepared for such situations. Guided by SOPs and prepared contingency plans, we worked step by step towards the resolution of the crisis.

In any crisis situation, communication is crucial to ensure everyone knows the situation, the current goal, and what must be done. And don't forget, in these high-pressure situations, we need to be fit not just mentally but also physically. We need people who are tough and won't break down as we resolve the problem.

I'm a big fan of resilience because it enables us to navigate complex situations and find solutions for practically any problem. And on those rare occasions when you encounter a problem you can't solve, you can simply manage the situation and live with it.

How to Balance Leadership Responsibilities with Personal Life

When trying to keep the proper balance between business and personal life, I have found that the Eisenhower Matrix, also known as the Urgent-Important Matrix, can be a great help. With this productivity tool, I am able to prioritize my tasks depending on how urgent and important they are. Tasks that are both urgent and important, I do them immediately. For those that are important but not urgent, I schedule them to be done later. Those that are urgent but not important, I delegate them to someone else if possible. Lastly, I will simply forget tasks that are not urgent and important and take them off the to-do list. This tool will make sure I will be devoting the limited time I have to what is urgent and important.

Naturally, the urgent and important tasks that are required to solve a crisis are at the top of my to-do list. I schedule the important but not urgent tasks of keeping myself in great shape. Thus, I have a schedule to follow in doing workouts every day in the morning and also in the evening—running, strength training, HIIT, and Krav Maga. I structure my day, deciding what is urgent and critical, and work on each task. Then, during the day, I make space for my diet and food and also for other personal life tasks within the boundaries and limits. Of course, I keep in mind that I must always be flexible and constantly adapt to the current situation, and I must remember that priorities can suddenly change and adjust accordingly.

How to Remain Motivated and Keep Going

This is a question that I ask myself every morning because it is a reality of life. There are days when we feel less motivated. That is why I always remind myself about my long-term goal, and this keeps me going. My long-term vision is to become the leading voice in global crisis management, and this has kept me going in the face of difficult problems and obstacles. I am also able to maintain my motivation by establishing new challenges, whether it is writing my upcoming book or breaking into new markets. Being motivated keeps me persistent, and this is fueled by my desire to achieve my vision of creating a legacy, not just in business but also in my personal life. This is the legacy of ensuring the people I mentor and my family are able to thrive long after I'm gone.

How My Understanding of Leadership Has Evolved Through the Years

Just like with my success journey, my understanding of leadership has been constantly evolving. At the start, I had to rely on natural leadership skills that gradually grew over time. In my experience, I learned that leadership is not about having control and constantly checking on various details. Instead, it's about trusting my team and empowering them to do their job. A true leader gives the task and responsibility to their trusted people and doesn't care how they do it. It is not about micromanaging the various details of the task. I just make sure to entrust the task to people who are upcoming leaders. What better way to train new leaders than by allowing them to practice the skills they have learned in real-life situations, and still be there in the background if further support is needed?

And just like I said at the start, it is about planning and preparation. Leaders need to deal with crisis situations, which is what they are paid to do, and this requires preparing and making adjustments whenever needed. You need to prepare the mission and then prepare the plan for its accomplishment. Always remember there is no plan etched in stone. A plan must be flexible and ready to adjust and adapt to the situation to ensure it will succeed. Oftentimes, all of the information needed is not available to ensure you have made the right decision. Never try to be perfect because you don't have 100 percent of the necessary information, but maybe it is only 80 percent, 70 percent, or even less.

A leader must always practice persistence every day because there are crucial stakes on a daily basis, allowing you to cope with high pressure all the time. And don't forget about communication. All that preparation and planning would be useless without ensuring the team members know the current situation, their goals, and what is required of them. Whenever there is a crisis situation, the first thing a leader has to do is acknowledge the existence of the problem, then gather the information needed to make the critical decision on what needs to be done. But always remember not to aim for perfection because this can paralyze you. You can make necessary changes at any time. You just need to keep going. Stop only from time to time to ensure you are headed in the right direction. What is important is to pursue your goal, whether in business or in life, relentlessly!

Summary

Crisis management and risk handling are essential for achieving success, whether in business or personal life. There are always uncertainties, and a leader may experience varying degrees of fear depending on the situation's severity. It is vital to manage that fear because only then can a leader think properly about what must be done to handle the crisis and find the appropriate solution. In my experience, a leader has to practice persistence every day because there is always strong pressure from responsibilities. I need to cope with that pressure all the time.

Success is a continuous journey. It is not something that can be achieved overnight, which is why we need to be persistent and able to adjust and adapt to the specific situations we find ourselves in and keep moving towards our goals. There are always surprises along the way, and people need to be prepared. Oftentimes, leaders need external support and guidance. That is why I write books and articles to share my knowledge and experience with people who have a burning desire to make things better. As we grow older, it is natural to want to leave a legacy by giving people the right tools to make them tough, mentally and physically, to navigate the challenges and crises they will face as they strive to achieve their goals.

Navigating Uncertainty: Lessons from Explorers, Entrepreneurs, and the Future

Aaron Poynton

Dr. Aaron Poynton is a best-selling author and seasoned entrepreneur with a rich background in navigating complex and uncertain environments. As the founder of several successful ventures, he has demonstrated a keen ability to leverage strategic insights and innovative thinking to drive growth and transformation.

Aaron holds advanced degrees in law, business, and political science. He has studied at prestigious institutions such as Duke University, Harvard Business School, and the London School of Economics. His expertise spans various industries, including technology, defense, and energy, where he has consistently applied his leadership and strategic planning to overcome challenges and seize opportunities. Aaron's approach is deeply rooted in the principles of adaptive intelligence and emotional mastery, enabling him to build resilient organizations that thrive in the face of disruption. With a commitment to fostering innovation and embracing calculated risks, he exemplifies the qualities of a modern leader who not only navigates uncertainty but uses it as a catalyst for growth and success. His work continues to inspire others to embrace change and lead with vision and purpose.

The year is 1914. Sir Ernest Shackleton and his crew aboard the *Endurance* are locked in the icy grip of the Weddell Sea, and their expedition to cross Antarctica is thwarted by the unforgiving power of nature. Their ship, trapped and slowly being crushed by the relentless pressure of the ice, becomes their prison. There is no rescue on the horizon, no satellite phone to call for help, and no detailed plan B for such a catastrophic turn of events. Shackleton, facing a blank canvas of a future, must navigate the unknown with courage, resourcefulness, and unwavering resolve.

His decisions, made in the face of unimaginable pressure and with the lives of his men hanging in the balance, became a masterclass in leadership under uncertainty—a lesson as relevant today as it was over a century ago.

Shackleton's story isn't just a thrilling tale of survival; it's a profound study of how to lead when the map has run out, and the only guide is instinct, experience, and an unyielding commitment to the well-being of those under your command. He made the impossible possible, transforming a potential tragedy into a testament to human resilience and the power of leadership.

The Deluge of Data and the Illusion of Control

Fast-forward to the twenty-first century. The 2008 financial crisis, the dot-com bubble, the unexpected rise and fall of cryptocurrencies, the COVID-19 pandemic—these events remind us that even the most sophisticated models can be blindsided by unforeseen circumstances such as the "black swan" events that defy prediction and reshape the landscape overnight. The world is a complex, adaptive system, and our attempts to impose linear predictions on its nonlinear reality often fall short. The illusion of control, fostered by the deluge of data, can be a dangerous trap, lulling us into a false sense of security while the ground shifts beneath our feet. The key is not to abandon data, but to understand its limitations and to cultivate the wisdom to discern signal from noise.

Leaders today are drowning in data. We have more information at our fingertips than ever before—market analyses, economic forecasts, consumer trends, competitor intelligence—all flowing in an unrelenting torrent. We live in the age of Big Data, where algorithms track our every click, sensors monitor global supply chains, and artificial intelligence sifts through mountains of information in search of meaningful patterns. Yet, paradoxically, this abundance of information often creates more confusion than clarity. We build sophisticated algorithms, deploy AI-powered analytics, and create real-time dashboards—all in the pursuit of predicting the future and controlling outcomes. But the future, as Shackleton discovered, remains stubbornly elusive.

Information Overload and the Paralysis of Analysis

The sheer volume of data available can be overwhelming, leading to a state of analysis paralysis. Leaders, faced with a mountain of spreadsheets, reports, and conflicting expert opinions, can become so fixated on analyzing every possible scenario that they fail to make timely decisions. This phenomenon is particularly prevalent in industries undergoing rapid transformation, such as technology, where the pace of innovation is relentless and the competitive landscape can shift dramatically in a matter of months. Consider the case of Nokia. Once a dominant player in the mobile phone market, Nokia possessed vast amounts of market data, consumer research, and technological expertise.

Yet, when faced with the disruptive force of the smartphone, spearheaded by Apple's iPhone, they hesitated, paralyzed by the potential implications of cannibalizing their existing business. Their over-reliance on analysis, coupled with a fear of the unknown and a reluctance to disrupt their established business model, ultimately cost them their market leadership. While data is essential, it cannot replace decisive action. Overthinking can be as dangerous as underthinking, especially in a rapidly changing environment. The ability to synthesize information, extract key insights from the data deluge, and make timely decisions based on imperfect information is crucial for navigating uncertainty.

The Art of Intuitive Leadership: The Dance Between Data and Instinct

In an era marked by constant change, intuition becomes a critical leadership skill. The most effective leaders understand that data is a tool, not a crutch. They cultivate a finely tuned instinct, honed by years of experience, that allows them to recognize patterns, assess risks, and make judgments even when the data is incomplete or contradictory. This isn't about abandoning data-driven decision-making; it's about recognizing its limitations and supplementing it with the wisdom that comes from experience and a deep understanding of human behavior.

Steve Jobs, with his uncanny ability to anticipate consumer desires, is a prime example. He didn't rely solely on market research; he trusted his intuition and his understanding of what people wanted even before they knew it themselves. This blend of data and instinct, of analysis and intuition, is the hallmark of effective leadership in uncertain times. It's about recognizing that data can inform, but it cannot replace the human element of judgment, vision, and the courage to take calculated risks. Leaders must learn to trust their gut, to listen to that inner voice that integrates experience, knowledge, and a deep understanding of the forces at play.

The Peril of Indecision: Why "Wait and See" Is Often the Worst Strategy

In the face of uncertainty, the most dangerous decision is often no decision at all. Waiting for perfect clarity and for all the data to align perfectly is a recipe for missed opportunities and eventual obsolescence. The world rewards those who act and are willing to take calculated risks and adjust course as needed.

Blockbuster's demise serves as a stark reminder of this principle. While Netflix disrupted the video rental industry with its innovative streaming model, Blockbuster hesitated, clinging to its brick-and-mortar stores and waiting for the market to "settle down." Their indecision and unwillingness to embrace the uncertainty of a new business model ultimately led to their downfall. They had the opportunity to acquire Netflix early on, but they dismissed the nascent streaming service as a niche market, a decision that would prove fatal.

In a rapidly changing world, inaction is often the biggest risk of all. The ability to make timely decisions, even with imperfect information, is crucial for survival and success. Leaders must cultivate the courage to act, embrace the inherent risks of innovation, and adapt their strategies as the landscape evolves.

Emotional Intelligence: The Human Element of Leadership

Navigating uncertainty requires more than just analytical skills and intuitive judgment; it demands emotional intelligence. Leaders must be able to read the emotional landscape of their organizations, understand the anxieties and aspirations of their teams, and build trust in a climate of uncertainty. They must project calm amidst the storm, inspire confidence when doubt prevails, and navigate complex interpersonal dynamics with grace and empathy. Satya Nadella's leadership at Microsoft provides a compelling example. He inherited a company that was struggling with internal divisions, a loss of market share, and had become somewhat complacent and resistant to change.

Nadella, through his emotionally intelligent leadership, fostered a culture of collaboration, trust, and shared purpose. He encouraged risk-taking and embraced a growth mindset, transforming Microsoft into a more agile and innovative organization. His success in revitalizing Microsoft stemmed not only from strategic brilliance but also from his ability to connect with people on an emotional level, to inspire them to embrace change, and to build a sense of shared purpose in the face of the unknown. He understood that navigating uncertainty requires a clear vision.

The Innovation Imperative: Embracing Risk as a Catalyst for Growth

In a rapidly evolving landscape, playing it safe is often the riskiest strategy. Companies that prioritize stability over innovation and cling to existing models in the face of changing market dynamics are destined for decline. Kodak's failure to embrace digital photography—despite inventing the technology—serves as a cautionary tale. Their reluctance to cannibalize their highly profitable film business blinded them to the disruptive potential of digital imaging. Conversely, Tesla's meteoric rise demonstrates the power of embracing uncertainty and challenging industry norms.

Elon Musk's willingness to take risks, bet on unproven technologies like electric vehicles and autonomous driving, and challenge conventional wisdom has propelled Tesla to the forefront of the automotive industry. He didn't wait for the market to validate his vision; he created the market. Innovation thrives on uncertainty. It requires a willingness to step outside your comfort zone—to experiment, fail, and learn from those failures. It requires a willingness to step outside your comfort zone, to experiment, fail, and learn, fostered by a culture that celebrates bold ideas, encourages experimentation, and sees failure as a valuable learning opportunity rather than a stigma.

Building Resilience: Adaptability as the Engine of Survival

Resilience is not simply about bouncing back from setbacks; it's about adapting, evolving, and learning from every experience. It's about building organizations that are agile, flexible, and capable of pivoting quickly in response to changing market conditions. SpaceX's early failures, followed by their remarkable successes, exemplify this principle. Each failed launch and explosion on the landing pad provided valuable lessons, fueling their relentless pursuit of innovation and their eventual mastery of reusable rocket technology.

Resilience requires a growth mindset—the belief that setbacks are not failures, but opportunities to learn and improve—supported by a culture that encourages experimentation, tolerates mistakes, and recognizes failure as a necessary stepping stone to success. In an uncertain world, adaptability is not just a desirable trait; it's the engine of survival and the key to long-term success. It's about building organizations that can not only withstand shocks but also learn and adapt, emerging stronger and more resilient from each challenge.

The New Leadership DNA: Traits for Thriving in Uncertainty

The leaders who thrive in uncertainty are not necessarily those who possess the most data or the most sophisticated analytical tools. They are those who possess a unique blend of qualities that enable them to navigate the unknown with confidence and wisdom. These qualities include:

- **Adaptive Intelligence:** The ability to learn and unlearn quickly, to adapt to changing circumstances, and to synthesize information from diverse sources. This requires a growth mindset, a willingness to embrace new ideas, and a commitment to continuous learning.
- **Calculated Risk-Taking:** The ability to take risks, but not recklessly. It's about assessing risks carefully, balancing boldness with prudence, and being comfortable with ambiguity.
- **Emotional Mastery:** The ability to manage one's emotions and to understand and influence the emotions of others. This includes self-awareness, empathy, and the skill to build trust and rapport.
- **Vision Beyond Chaos:** The ability to see beyond the immediate challenges and to maintain a long-term perspective. It's about recognizing patterns in chaos, identifying opportunities in disruption, and preserving a clear sense of direction even when the path forward is unclear.

The Future of Decision-Making: Embracing the Art of the Possible

Traditional decision-making models, based on linear projections and the assumption of predictable outcomes, are increasingly inadequate in today's complex and rapidly changing world. The future of decision-making will require new approaches that embrace uncertainty, encourage experimentation, and prioritize adaptability. This includes:

- **Faster Decision Cycles:** The ability to make decisions quickly, even with imperfect information, is becoming increasingly critical. This requires streamlined processes, decentralized decision-making authority, and a willingness to embrace calculated risks.
- **More Flexible Strategic Planning:** Traditional long-term strategic plans are often obsolete before they are implemented. The future of strategic planning will require greater agility, adaptability, and a willingness to adjust course as needed.
- **Enhanced Pattern Recognition:** The ability to identify emerging trends, see patterns in seemingly random events, and anticipate future developments will become increasingly valuable. This requires a combination of data analysis, intuitive judgment, and a deep understanding of the forces shaping the future.
- **Stronger Emotional Intelligence:** As the pace of change accelerates and the world becomes more complex, the ability to manage emotions, build trust, and navigate interpersonal dynamics will become even more critical for effective leadership.

Embracing the Unknown as the Path to Innovation

The future belongs to those who can navigate uncertainty with confidence, wisdom, and adaptability. Like Shackleton in the Antarctic, modern leaders must combine courage with judgment, intuition with analysis, and vision with execution. Success isn't about eliminating uncertainty—it's about thriving within it. This new landscape demands leadership that embraces ambiguity as an opportunity rather than a threat. The path forward isn't about having all the answers—it's about asking better questions, building resilient organizations, and maintaining a clear vision amid chaos. In doing so, we don't just survive uncertainty—we use it as a catalyst for growth and innovation.

The greatest opportunities often lie hidden in the fog of the unknown. Those who learn to navigate this fog with skill and confidence will be the ones who shape the future. The time for bold, decisive leadership isn't when the path is clear—it's when the way forward seems most uncertain. It's in these moments of ambiguity and not knowing that true leadership emerges, forging a path not only through the uncertainty, but also because of it.

Grit, Hustle, and Humanity: Lessons in Resilience and Growth

Darius Alexander 'Dman' Ross

Darius A. Ross is a serial entrepreneur who has faced some of life's toughest challenges, from homelessness to urban warfare. These experiences have shaped his tactical and strategic skills, enabling him to succeed in both small businesses and Fortune 500 corporations. Ross has built and scaled multiple businesses, some thriving, others failing—each providing invaluable lessons. Drawing on these experiences, he now runs a consulting practice focused on high-net-worth individuals, families, and aspiring entrepreneurs.

Ross is also an accomplished author and a contributing writer to the USA National Bestseller Leadership DNA Anthology. He is currently working on his upcoming solo book, which promises to further expand on his unique perspectives on entrepreneurship and success.

Ross offers three core programs: Urban No BS; Grind, Refine, and Lootnomics; and HGDR (Hustle, Grind, Define, Refine). These programs are not for everyone; they're designed for individuals who are determined to achieve greatness, massive profits, and sustainable success. Whether as a coach, consultant, author, or speaker, Ross provides the tools, mindset, and strategies to help clients reach their full potential and excel in both business and life.

I embrace a comprehensive and dynamic approach to leadership and success, rooted in five key traits: grit, hustle, stamina, intuition, and foresight. Grit, as John Wayne defined it, is "making a decision and standing by it, doing what must be done." Wayne, an iconic figure in American cinema, believed in standing firm in the face of challenges and doing what needed to be done, even when it was difficult. Grit reflects a willingness to engage fully, collaborate with the team, and tackle challenges head-on.

Hustle, the second trait, signifies relentless focus and precision, ensuring that everyone remains aligned with goals and expectations. Stamina represents the endurance required to sustain efforts over time, demonstrating resilience and a commitment to achieving long-term results. Intuition, as I define it, is akin to "woman's intuition"—the ability to anticipate events before they unfold. Lastly, this intuition pairs with foresight, which involves analyzing potential outcomes and taking proactive steps to prevent issues, effectively reducing the need for damage control.

Success Requires Adaptability

Over time, I have come to realize that success requires adaptability in both business and life. It involves the ability to adjust to trends, concepts, and the ever-changing nature of humanity. There was a challenging period when my company faced significant difficulties—something akin to "hitting a brick wall"—and we had to manage pending bankruptcies for multiple businesses. During this time, we made critical adjustments to adapt and stay afloat, highlighting the importance of flexibility in times of adversity.

We must recognize that the world is evolving, and I want to place my experiences within the broader context of societal and cultural shifts over the past fifty-nine years, transitioning from rigid corporate norms to the embrace of inclusion and diversity in the workplace. Coming from a structured corporate environment that was very cut-and-dry, I found myself forced to adapt to change. Traditional corporate cultures, like those at IBM, AT&T, and similar institutions, emphasized conformity in appearance and discouraged deviations from established norms. However, success requires adaptability, compelling me to embrace a new, more fluid, and dynamic world.

Most Important Influences on My Approach to Leadership and Persistence

Two influential figures in business history have profoundly shaped my approach to leadership and persistence: Henry Kravis of KKR and Jack Welch of GE. Henry Kravis built a private equity firm from scratch, transforming it into a global investment behemoth. Jack Welch, on the other hand, took GE and expanded its various divisions, molding it into today's renowned, colossal conglomerate. I admire them for their extraordinary ability to transform companies, whether in private equity or industrial sectors, into formidable entities through strategic vision and innovation.

Another crucial influence on me is the cultural evolution in India, China, and Africa. I recall visiting China in the 1990s and now contrasting the modest agricultural landscapes of the past with the rapid industrial and economic rise of these regions, which have since transformed into global powerhouses. This transformation embodies the same principles of growth and adaptability that I observed in the work of Kravis and Welch.

The remarkable progress and global influence of cultures once categorized as "third world" are truly astounding. These nations have undergone profound transformations, achieving levels of economic and cultural development that now position them as leaders in the global corporate landscape. Witnessing this shift, I have observed the dynamic nature of global power structures and the increasingly significant role these formerly underestimated nations now play in shaping the corporate world. Their evolution exemplifies adaptability, resilience, and growth, challenging outdated perceptions and redefining their place on the global stage.

My Approach to Handling Challenges

One significant obstacle I had to overcome was impending bankruptcy, which required me to navigate challenging negotiations with creditors and banks. My approach centered on a "loss principle," where I assessed my own position as rock bottom—having already accepted my losses—and then focused on framing the creditors' potential losses as even greater. I emphasized the importance of shifting perspectives, placing my counterparts in the same challenging position I faced. By doing so, I fostered a shared understanding of mutual loss, which opened the door for collaborative negotiations to find a solution that minimized damage for both parties. This strategy relied on my ability to effectively communicate the reality of the situation, encouraging all sides to work together rather than face even worse outcomes.

I use the metaphor of water to illustrate the importance of emotional regulation, self-awareness, and thoughtful leadership. Water, when pushed, can become volatile and violent, yet remains calm and cool when undisturbed. I draw a parallel between this behavior and my own emotional state, acknowledging the need to confront personal challenges and maintain self-control. I've developed the ability to recognize and manage moments of heightened emotion or stress. Finding ways to stay composed under pressure is crucial for leading effectively, whether it's a team or a company. By avoiding reactive, knee-jerk decisions and instead taking time to assess situations thoughtfully, a more strategic and balanced approach to leadership can be achieved.

In addition, it is important to maintain a clear boundary between personal life and business life, as the two can influence each other in ways that may not always be beneficial. By keeping these areas separate, I am able to achieve greater clarity and make better decisions. To help maintain this balance, I engage in activities such as practicing martial arts like Krav Maga from Israel or Muay Thai from Thailand, people-watching, yoga, and spending time in nature. These activities not only bring personal fulfillment but also enhance my ability to understand and connect with others, a skill I consider central to effective leadership.

I believe that to be a great leader, one must first be a great follower. This means meeting people where they are, understanding their perspectives, and building connections rooted in empathy. By combining this people-centered approach with a commitment to maintaining boundaries, I strive to lead with clarity and intentionality, which involves being mindful of one's actions and the impact they have on others or on the situation at hand.

Experiencing and Learning from Failure

One huge disappointment I experienced was missing out on a million-dollar deal with a major corporation after a year of effort trying to buy its subsidiary, only to see a much larger, billion-dollar opportunity emerge soon after. This experience led to a deeper appreciation of timing and understanding that some events are simply not meant to happen at a particular moment. My candid moment of questioning, even frustration, toward higher powers underscores the very human tendency to seek meaning in challenging times. However, I have come to embrace the concept of karma (cause and effect) and timing, recognizing that my good actions and efforts will eventually align with positive outcomes. This mindset of trusting the process and accepting life's realities allows me to move forward with grace and resilience.

My Advice to Upcoming Leaders on Mastering Persistence and Achieving Success

I acknowledge that life can get f***** up, difficult, unpredictable, and often uncomfortable. My focus is on accepting reality and being practical with expectations, rather than chasing an idealized or perfect vision of life. A quote from Notorious B.I.G.—"on the road to riches and diamond rings, real people do real things"—reinforces the idea that authenticity and action are key to navigating life's challenges. There's also an element of resilience: by laughing at the absurdity or struggles of life, one can find strength and understanding. Ultimately, it's about embracing life's imperfections, staying grounded, and pushing forward despite the discomfort.

I want to emphasize to future leaders that our greatest challenges—our biggest demons—often stem from within: our own pride, overconfidence, or sense of self-importance. I urge you to "leave ego at the door" and embrace humility and self-awareness, understanding that arrogance can alienate others, especially employees or colleagues. Beware that while ego-driven decisions might achieve short-term financial gains, they can result in long-term consequences, such as strained relationships, loss of trust, and ultimately harm to the organization or team. Instead, prioritize authenticity, collaboration, and respect over self-centeredness.

To stay motivated and maintain persistence over the long term, remember that discomfort is a natural part of the journey to success, and these challenging experiences ultimately lead to growth and achievement. Based on my experience, my youthful ambition initially drove me to aim for the "top of the food chain," where everything seemed perfectly aligned. However, over time, I realized that success is shaped by factors such as timing, the wisdom gained through life experiences, and the ability to expect the unexpected. The sense of invincibility or overconfidence you may feel in your youth will eventually give way to humility and a broader perspective as you mature.

I want to emphasize the importance of learning from others, especially those with more experience, and being willing to adjust and pivot when circumstances require it. The essence of what I would like young people aspiring to be leaders to learn lies in resilience: not allowing setbacks or challenges to defeat you, but rather using them as opportunities to adapt and ultimately persevere.

The Irreplaceable Value of Humanity

My final insight is a reminder of the irreplaceable value of humanity. While technology like AI is powerful and transformative, businesses ultimately rely on people. When systems fail, it is human ingenuity and effort that prevail. I advocate staying grounded, prioritizing human relationships, and ensuring that the human element remains central to every endeavor.

I had also experienced a shift in mindset—from perceiving younger generations as adversaries to seeing them as valuable contributors who bring fresh perspectives and innovations. It is important to embrace the insights younger individuals offer, particularly when it comes to rethinking traditional practices and leveraging technology in transformative ways.

At the same time, I want to underscore the responsibility of experienced leaders to pass on wisdom, lessons, and historical context to guide and empower the next generation. It's not about clinging to old ways, but about balancing innovation with the foundations that have brought progress so far. The call for wisdom as a guiding principle stresses the importance of thoughtful decision-making, ensuring that changes are made with intention and purpose.

Remember that we are living in a period of significant change, both in society and leadership. The ability to adapt, collaborate across generations, and remain focused on humanity's shared challenges is crucial for navigating the complexities of the modern world.

What Keeps Me Driven Despite Challenges and Setbacks

As we progress in our careers and lives—particularly into middle age— our goals and hunger for opportunities may shift. Take note that success requires not just drive, but also vision, focus, and an understanding of one's limitations. It's a more measured approach to ambition, informed by wisdom and past experiences.

I emphasize integration, both in systems and in people, and point out the importance of collaboration and cohesion within organizations. It's not just about acquiring companies or talents, but about effectively combining and aligning them to function as a unified whole.

Conclusion and Final Thoughts

In conclusion, I would like to reflect on a global and inclusive perspective on humanity's future. I acknowledge the growing interconnectedness of the world, emphasizing that traditional divides—whether ideological, cultural, or geographical—are becoming increasingly irrelevant in the face of shared challenges and opportunities. Rapid population growth in regions like India, Africa, and Southeast Asia, coupled with projections that the global population could reach ten to twenty billion by 2050, highlights the importance of recognizing and integrating diverse talents and cultures into a cohesive global framework.

As a nation of immigrants, America serves as a reminder of its multicultural foundation and the need to embrace this diversity as a strength. The phrase "the yellowing and browning of America" highlights demographic shifts toward a more diverse population, urging people to adapt to and celebrate this reality. I also stress the importance of representation and the responsibility to acknowledge and uplift the cultures and individuals who will shape the future.

Ultimately, I call for a forward-thinking approach to global integration, focusing on humanity's collective progress rather than individual or nationalistic interests. This vision emphasizes unity, adaptability, and shared responsibility in navigating a rapidly evolving world.

Success Requires No Talent

Dr. Prasad S. Kodukula,
PMP, PgMP, PMI-ACP, DASM, DASSM, BCES

Dr. Prasad S. Kodukula is a USA Today best-selling author, PMI Fellow, thought leader, and entrepreneur. A global ambassador for project management, Dr. Kodukula has lectured in nearly 50 countries and worked with more than 40 Fortune 100 companies in every one of the 11 S&P industrial sectors. He is an adjunct faculty member at the University of Chicago and Illinois Tech. He also teaches how to recover troubled projects for NASA.

As co-founder and CEO of Kodukula & Associates, Inc. and NeoChloris, Inc., he leads firms in project management and renewable energy, respectively. Recognized three times by the Project Management Institute as "Best of the Best in Project Management," he has received multiple accolades, including the Illinois Tech Alumni Association Professional Achievement Award and honors from the US Environmental Protection Agency and the States of Arizona, Kansas, and Illinois for his outstanding leadership in education/training, environmental improvement, and innovation. An accomplished author, Dr. Kodukula has co-authored or contributed to 12 books and more than 40 articles and holds four US patents.

The title of this chapter—Success Requires *No Talent*—is bold and provocative by design. It's meant to stop you in your tracks and challenge the enduring myth that success is reserved for the naturally gifted. But here's the truth: Contrary to the provocative title of the chapter, everyone has *some* talent. We're all born with different starting points along what I call the talent continuum— not one of us begins at zero. Yet, wherever you start, talent alone doesn't determine your destiny.

That's because talent, at its core, is just a blueprint—an outline of potential. But blueprints don't build anything. You still need the tools, the process, and the discipline to bring that design to life. That process is built on skills, and unlike innate talent, skills can be developed. As you build your skills, you often refine and elevate your natural ability, which becomes, over time, acquired talent.

This chapter lives intentionally within the broader theme of *Success DNA*. If success truly has a genetic code, I didn't inherit mine—I built it. The "genes" that shaped my journey weren't gifts; they were hard-earned lessons. In this chapter, I'll share the eight secrets that acted as my personal success genes—unwritten rules I uncovered in hindsight, practiced over time, and now want to pass on.

You don't need to be extraordinary to succeed. You just need to be deliberate, especially in learning the things no one ever taught you.

My Background

I wasn't born into success. I wasn't a child prodigy or at the top of my class. I didn't show early signs of genius, leadership, or creativity. By most standards, I was "average."

My parents, four of my siblings, and I lived together in a small one-room apartment in India. Luxuries were nonexistent. My father worked a low wage job to support us. From the outside, my life looked full of limitations. But inside, I carried a quiet conviction: I wanted more. And I had a dream. Not to have more money or things, but to come to America, pursue an education, and create a better life. That dream made all the difference.

I wasn't gifted in school. I struggled, nearly flunked out of college, and had no special talent in sports, music, or art. Years later, I earned a PhD, became a best-selling author, built multiple businesses, earned certifications, and traveled the world coaching others.

What changed?

I started learning—deliberately. I learned how to set goals, develop a strategy, act boldly, take risks, focus, and persist. I didn't succeed because of any special talent. I succeeded by building a set of skills through practice and discipline.

Later, people assumed I must have always been talented. But they didn't see the failures, the doubts, or the slow progress. What they were seeing were the results of what I now call my eight secrets.

These weren't taught in classrooms. I discovered them in retrospect through lived experience. They're not magic—but they are powerful.

Secret #1: Live Life by Design, Not by Default

Some people know what they want to be when they grow up—from an early age, they're set on becoming a doctor, an artist, or a pilot. But most of us aren't like that. We drift for a while, unsure of our purpose. And that's okay—*as long as we don't stay on autopilot forever.* Even without a master plan, we must begin taking deliberate steps.

For much of my early life, I was drifting—not because I lacked ambition, but because I lacked clarity. My parents hoped I'd become a doctor, so I pursued biology in college. But my grades were dismal, and medical school quickly slipped out of reach. I didn't have a backup plan. I was simply moving forward by default.

The one thing I did know? My dream of going to America—fuzzy as it was—became my anchor. I didn't have a detailed blueprint, but I took intentional steps: I applied to graduate programs, leaned on my uncle's guidance, and eventually found my way to Cornell University for graduate school. The journey wasn't smooth. I struggled. I switched fields—from biology to education to environmental science to engineering in college and then to management during my professional career. But each decision nudged my life toward purpose.

Clarity isn't required, but direction is. Design your next step, and success will follow.

You don't need the full blueprint—just lay the first brick and keep building, one intentional step at a time.

Secret #2: Set Goals, Shape Strategy

After arriving in America, my next goal was clear: Earn a PhD. But clarity alone wasn't enough—I needed a strategy.

At Cornell, I entered a graduate engineering program alongside classmates with engineering degrees while I came from a biology and education background. The first few semesters were brutal, and I nearly failed. But I refused to give up.

I worked harder than ever. I built a study schedule, focused on the fundamentals, sought help from mentors, and slowly gained ground. Against the odds, I earned a master's degree in environmental engineering. But just short of my PhD, I had no choice but to leave—I could no longer afford the tuition, fees, and basic cost of living. I couldn't even afford a flight home—went seven years without seeing my parents.

That setback hurt. But I didn't give up. With my uncle's help (again), I transferred to another university (Illinois Institute of Technology), recalibrated my plan, and completed my PhD. Along the way, I immersed myself in extra-curricular activities, led student teams, and built the leadership skills that would later shape my career.

That experience taught me how powerful it is to define a goal and pursue it with intention. Set goals, but also shape your strategy as you go.

In today's volatile, uncertain, complex, and ambiguous (VUCA) world, flexibility matters especially. Persistence is still important—but so is the ability to pivot.

Strategy isn't about rigid plans—it's about learning, adjusting, and moving forward.

Secret #3: Practice "Less Is More"

When I first considered starting my business, I was full of energy and ideas. I made a list of thirteen different things I wanted to do. It felt exciting, but also overwhelming. I wasn't making progress and was burning out fast. Then I met with a career coach who told me, "You're not lacking ideas—you're lacking focus. Choose one. Go all in."

That was my lightbulb moment. I learned that focus is essential. The more you subtract, the more you can concentrate on what matters. I launched my first company soon after that conversation, and I've carried that lesson with me ever since.

"Less is more" isn't just a saying—it's a strategy. It means knowing what to cut, what to ignore, and where to go all in. It's about choosing the vital few over the trivial many, applying the 80/20 rule to your energy, time, and attention.

Success isn't about doing everything; it's about focusing on the right things—and ignoring the rest.

Secret #4: Act Boldly, Risk Wisely

An object at rest stays at rest—unless acted upon. Newton wasn't just describing physics; he was describing people.

Inertia is the enemy of progress in life. We change our situation by moving decisively and deliberately. When I lost my job at an engineering firm, I didn't stay stuck. Instead, I took action. Fast.

I boldly moved back to Chicago, believing the city would open doors. During my previous job, I'd discovered a love for public speaking, so I set myself a new goal: to build a speaking and consulting career—traveling the world and making an impact. Chicago, with its energy and global access, became my launchpad.

Success often requires doing what others won't—taking a risk not because it's reckless, but because it's grounded in purpose. And when you take risks, it's important to consider both the likelihood of things going wrong and the impact if they do—so you can manage those risks accordingly. I was afraid I might not survive in just one business, so I started two: project management and green technologies, both areas I deeply love. If one failed, I could rely on the other. Thankfully, both thrived.

Take action. Take risks. Test the path. You'll figure it out along the way. Secret #5: Put People First

Success Secret #5 is about something we rarely learn in school—people skills. Yet in the real world, these skills often matter more than technical knowledge. I learned that the hard way.

At the beginning of my career at the engineering firm I mentioned earlier, my boss gave me a "C" on my annual review, calling me "Jekyll and Hyde." The client loved my results, but my teammates hated working with me. I had strong technical skills, but I was burning people out. That moment stung—but it also woke me up. I needed to improve my "emotional intelligence."

So, I went to work—not on the projects, but on myself. I borrowed books and audio tapes on communication, team building, leadership, and general people skills. I attended seminars. I listened, practiced, and improved. Eventually, I became an associate partner at the engineering firm.

Since then, I've worked with people across the globe. Today's workforce is multi-national, multi-generational, multi-ethnic, multi-gender—what I call multi-X. To thrive, you need people skills. I use a model I call LOVE: Listen, Open (open-minded), Value (recognizing others' worth), and Empathize.

Put people first, and you won't just succeed. You'll help others succeed with you.

Secret #6: Seize Serendipity

A routine flight changed the course of my life.

In 1995, while traveling for work, a conversation unfolded with Susan, a stranger sitting across the aisle. After we landed, we had a quick meal at Applebee's, where I learned she was a motivational speaker with a top business skills training company. I told her that I had entertained the idea of becoming a public speaker. Without hesitation, she offered to introduce me to her team.

That introduction launched a 30-year speaking career, taking me to over 50 countries. Most people call it luck. But serendipity isn't just luck—it's a spark. And that spark only grows when you're curious enough to notice it and bold enough to act.

Opportunities are everywhere—but they rarely announce themselves. You don't wait for serendipity. You help create it. And when it knocks, you answer the door.

Secret #7: Embrace Failure

Treat setbacks as stepping stones—not stop signs—on the path to success. Failure has followed me throughout my career—flopped products, rejected pitches, lost client bids, the list goes on. But I never let failure stop me. Instead, I ask, *What can I learn? How can this make me better?* One of my most meaningful failures—a seemingly minor one— occurred during a workshop I delivered in South Africa. After four days of my teaching, a participant asked for her money back. In 30 years of teaching thousands, it was the only time that ever happened. Her reason? She believed one essential element was missing. And honestly, she was right. It was a failure on my part. Plain and simple. I could've dismissed her or become defensive. Instead, I listened. Reflected. And eventually, I wrote a book based on the very idea she had challenged me with.

Failure doesn't have to be dramatic to be important. Sometimes, even the smallest stumbles hold the biggest lessons—if we're willing to face them with humility. Own them with no excuses.

Learn from failure. Lean into it. Let it shape you, not shame you.

Secret #8: Be a Student for Life—and of Life

My father, part of the "Greatest Generation," held one job and skill set throughout his entire career. But today, Generation Z will likely have an average of fifteen different jobs over their lifetime, many requiring entirely new skills. In today's fast-changing world, knowledge quickly becomes outdated as technologies and skill requirements evolve.

We must become lifelong learners—not just to stay relevant, but to continue growing and thriving.

Learn well. Grow well. Live well.

Learning has always been my core value. I dedicate at least one hour each day reading, reflecting, and broadening my perspective. I make it a point to keep learning—new skills, fresh perspectives, and evolving practices—not just to stay sharp, but to grow in my work and serve others more meaningfully.

That daily habit reflects my belief in learning, one rooted in a concept from Zen Buddhism called *Shoshin*, or "beginner's mind." It means embracing a novice's mindset—curious, humble, and eager to learn, no matter how much you already know.

Moreover, it's not just about being a student for life. It's about being a student *of* life—recognizing the lessons hidden in ordinary moments, conversations, missteps, and unexpected turns.

Life is a classroom. Show up curious. Show up often. And keep learning.

Closing

People often believe that success stems from talent—and no talent means no success. But that's a myth. Yes, we all start with some degree of talent— but what matters more is what we choose to do with it. Talent might give you a head start, but it doesn't guarantee the finish line. I've never considered myself extraordinarily talented, yet I've built a life I'm deeply grateful for— step by step, choice by choice—by leaning into the very skills I've shared in this chapter.

That's why I say success requires no talent. It demands something greater: a mindset, a series of choices, and a commitment to growth. Talent matters, but not as much as people think. That's the deeper message behind the title of this chapter: It's about liberating success from the myth that talent is everything.

The eight secrets are not mere theories—they are real-life lessons forged through trial, failure, perseverance, and faith. And while they come from my own journey, I've seen them echoed in the lives of other successful people. These aren't just my truths—they're shared patterns of lasting success.

Success isn't a destination—it's a journey. I've been on that journey for as long as I can remember, and I hope to continue walking it for as long as I'm able. And wherever you are—starting out, starting over, or somewhere in between—remember, you don't have to be extraordinary to succeed. You just have to begin.

So, start today.

Start with intention.

And build your own Success DNA.

www.ingramcontent.com/pod-product-compliance
Lightning Source LLC
Chambersburg PA
CBHW071422210326
41597CB00020B/3622